Constantine
High Cross
Polwheveral
Port Navas
Scott's Quay
Merthen
Helford Passage
①
Helford
Bosahan
Frenchman's Creek
Kestle
St Anthony-in-Meneage
②
Nare Point
Manaccan
Flushing & Gillan
Nare Head
M e n e a g e

St Martin
Trelowarren
Newtown
Tregidden
Porthallow

Porthkerris

Traboe
St Keverne
Porthoustock
Manacle Point
Traboe Cross
B3293
Rosenithon
Godrevy Cove
B3293
36
Roskilly's
Manacles

ONHILLY SHEET
C r o u s a D o w n s
Main Dale
B3294
The Grove
Lowland Point
Top of ophiolite sequence

Trelan Gwenter
Moho
Coverack

Poldowrian
CROUSA SHEET
Chynhalls Point
Arrowan
Treleaver
Mears Beach (Porthbeer Cove)
Bottom of ophiolite sequence
Gwendtreath
Black Head

Kuggar
Kennack Sands
Downas Cove
Poltesco (Carleon) Cove
Lankidden
Ruan Minor
Cadgwith
Boat trips (seasonal)

Devil's Frying Pan
olwidden

Church Cove (Landewednack)

Lizard Wireless Station
ass Point

Housel Bay
MAN O'WAR SHEET

● Approximate extent of Lizard thrust sheet under the sea

Get your bearings
The Lizard

Kilometres
0 1 2 3 4 5

0 1 2 3
Miles

Credits & Acknowledgements

Many thanks to Robin Shail for his great help,
criticisms & suggestions for the section on the geology of the Lizard
& to Paul Gainey and Ray Lawman for their help with the flora of the Lizard.

Watercolour illustrations: Bridgitte Livesley & Chema Cruz.
Trelan mirror: © The Trustees of the British Museum. All rights reserved.
Pillow lava p15 OAR/National Undersea Research Program (NURP).
Picture of deformed & sheared gabbro at Lankidden p75 by Robin Shail

The Cornish place name translations used in this book are from:
Cornish Place-name Elements by OJ Padel

Shipwreck information is largely drawn from:
Cornish Shipwrecks, The South Coast by Richard Larn & Clive Carter

Archaeological information is largely drawn from:
Cornwall Historic Environment Record & Cornish Archaeology
St Keverne Historic Landscape Assessment Cornwall Archaeological Unit
Helford Estuary Historic Audit Cornwall Archaeological Unit
Goon, hal, cliff & croft: the archaeology and landscape of West Cornwall's rough ground
Cornwall Council & English Heritage

Geological & natural history information is largely drawn from:
Cornwall's Geology & Scenery – An Introduction by Colin Bristow
Igneous Rocks of South West England by PA Floyd, CS Exley & MT Styles
Geology of the Lizard & Meneage by the British Geological Survey
Geology of Britain Viewer at the British Geological Survey website
British Geological Survey 1:50,000 & 1:250,000 maps
Serpentine & Its Vegetation by RR Brooks
A Natural History of the Lizard Peninsula by Jean Lawman
British Plant Communities Vol 2 Mires & Heaths by JS Rodwell
Flora of Cornwall by Colin French, Rosaline Murphy & Mary Atkinson
The Heaths of the Cornish Serpentine by DE Coombe & LC Frost

First published in 1999 as *The Map & Guide to Exploring the Lizard Peninsula*
This edition © Neil Reid & Friendly Guides 2013

ISBN
978-1-904645-06-1 (Paperback)
4th revised edition

MIX
Paper from
responsible sources
FSC® C023242

The Friendly Guides logo is a trademark of the Reid Partnership
1 St Mary's Terrace, Penzance, Cornwall, TR18 4DZ
Tel: 01736 369194 Email: info@friendly-guides.com
www.friendly-guides.com

Designed, published & printed in Cornwall

West Cornwall

The Lizard Guidebook

Helford, Helston, Porthleven, Mullion

4th Edition

Exploring Cornwall & Scilly
No. 3

The handsome nodding flowers of Great Burnet at the Earth Station on Goonhilly Downs. In Cornwall, Great Burnet is almost completely confined to the Lizard. Elsewhere in the UK it's a plant of river meadows, using its long rhizomes (underground stems) to survive prolonged flooding. The poorly draining serpentine soils of the Lizard seem to mimic its usual habitat.

Contents

Looking over Housel Bay to Pen Olver. These lovely blue/grey rocks are Landewednack schists. They were once lava that spilled onto an old ocean floor but have been stretched and recrystallised by the earth movements that thrust the Lizard onto Cornwall.

The Lizard
Beauty & the bleak

I KNOW OF NO OTHER PLACE IN CORNWALL, or for that matter in the UK, that has such a singular mix of ingredients as the Lizard. There's a savage and intimidating bleakness to the black serpentine cliffs at **Gew-graze** and **The Rill** and yet at **Carleon Cove** and **Housel Bay** you'll find a visual and sensory richness that can take your breath away – the aquamarine sea, the pebbles of every colour, the astonishing variety of plants. Cast a closer eye on the pebbles at **Pystyll Ogo** or **Coverack Cove** and a kaleidoscopic world reveals itself; drop to your knees on the coast path or on the downs and another order of richness unfolds – a world of miniature plants found nowhere else in Britain like *Fringed Rupture-wort* and *Land Quillwort*.

The Lizard is recognisably Cornish in its buildings and place names but in other aspects, in its scenery, rocks and plants, it can seem strikingly unusual and alien. For instance, there are odd, abrupt transitions between farmland and barren heath; a weird tabletop flatness to the downs and cliffs at **Vellan Head**; and at its heart on **Goonhilly Downs** is a place that appears to have turned its back on humans altogether. This is certainly Cornwall, but not as we know it.

The explanation for this strangeness lies squarely beneath your feet. On the Lizard, Mother Nature has reluctantly given up an unusual medley of igneous and metamorphic rocks that are only rarely found on dry land and properly belong in the Earth's oceanic crust and underlying mantle. It's these rare rocks that shape the distinctive character of the Lizard. The most unusual is **serpentinite** (commonly called **serpentine**). It's a rock seldom found at the Earth's surface, one more at home in the huge pressures and temperatures of the Earth's interior and so alien it has an ecology all of its own. In the first part of this book we'll look at these remarkable rocks – conveniently on display as polished beach pebbles – and then at the unusual habitats that are associated with them.

A basalt pebble on the beach at Pystyll Ogo near Lizard Point. Basalt dykes often have a uniform texture, but occasionally larger crystals that grow slowly in the main magma chamber are ejected to form these beautiful pebbles.

Gabbro

Basalt dyke

Man O'War Gneiss

Rocks of the Lizard

A sweetshop treat full of gobstopper colours

S IT ON A LIZARD BEACH LIKE **Coverack, Kennack, Carleon, Kynance** or **Pystyll Ogo** and you can't help but notice the great variety of colourful pebbles at your feet. Of course, there are lots of places in Cornwall where you can happily while away the hours combing the beach for shells and stones but nowhere comes close to having the marvellous variety, colour and texture of pebbles here. For beachcombers, the Lizard is a sweetshop treat full of gobstopper colours and dolly mix shapes.

The origin of the Lizard rocks puzzled geologists for many decades. In fact, it remained a mystery for more than a century after the rocks were first described in detail. It just wasn't clear why these unusual, colourful and contrasting rocks were attached to the far end of Cornwall – a county otherwise made up of straightforwardly familiar rocks like slate and granite.

We now recognise that the Earth has two distinct types of outer layer or lithosphere – oceanic and continental. Oceanic lithosphere is thin, dense and heavy. Continental lithosphere tends to be thicker and slightly less dense, it's therefore more buoyant and because of this, sits at higher elevations. This explains why continental lithosphere makes up most of the dry land and underlies most shallow seas like the English Channel, but dense oceanic lithosphere forms at low points at the Earth's surface and is usually covered by deep oceans.

In the normal course of events, oceanic lithosphere, which is what most of the Lizard is, doesn't make it onto dry land at all. It's formed out-of-sight under the sea at mid-ocean ridges, and consumed beneath the sea in deep sea trenches, where it's drawn back into the deep mantle to be recycled. This 'invisibility' explains why the origin of the Lizard rocks remained a puzzle for so long. It was only with the advent of plate tectonic theory in the late 1960s that a mechanism for incorporating slices of ocean floor between colliding continents was widely accepted. Before that, few people could accept that the Earth was in such restless motion, creating and destroying oceans by rifting continents apart and then forcing them together again.

The beach at Carleon (Poltesco) Cove is full of beautiful pebbles – a dark green lightly serpentinised peridotite (fresh serpentine), a deep red weathered serpentine, pink Kennack Gneiss & varieties of gabbro. The building below was part of the Lizard Serpentine Company's workshop. From 1853 they shipped serpentine mantelpieces, columns & ornaments to the palaces, banks & mansions of London.

Fresh serpentine

Gabbro

Kennack Gneiss

Red serpentine

Purple Loosestrife

So what caused this slice of oceanic lithosphere to become stranded in West Cornwall sandwiched between two continents? Well, 370 million years ago the Lizard was part of an ocean floor when it was caught up in a gigantic collision between two continents, **Gondwana** to the south (present-day Africa, South America and southern Europe) and **Laurasia** to the north (present-day North America, Greenland, northern Europe and most of Britain and Ireland). As the continents were forced together they overrode and destroyed the **Rheic Ocean** that once separated them. Slithers of oceanic lithosphere were caught up and entombed in a continental mountain range. It's one of those thin slices of oceanic lithosphere that makes up the colourful rocks and pebbles of the Lizard.

Oceanic lithosphere often has a characteristic vertical sequence of rock types called an *ophiolite*. Starting on the ocean floor and moving down into the Earth they are:

- OCEAN SEDIMENTS – a thin layer on the ocean floor
- BASALT – from 0–3 kilometres down
- GABBRO – from 3–7 kilometres down
- PERIDOTITE (serpentine) from 7–70 kilometres down

If you keep this simple sequence of rocks in mind as you walk across the Lizard you can identify which part of the oceanic lithosphere you are on and how far 'inside' the Earth you are. So for instance, when you look at **Mullion Island** you are looking at basalt lava erupted onto the sea floor, at **Godrevy Cove** you're on gabbro that cooled a few kilometres below the ocean floor itself, and at **Coverack** you're on the boundary between the gabbro and peridotite, about 7 kilometres down. Rocks like gabbro and basalt don't have to be formed in the ocean however, what's really unusual about the Lizard, and gives it away as a slice of ocean lithosphere, is that almost half of its area (about 50km^2) is made up of **mantle peridotite** or **serpentinite**. This is a rare and unusual rock to find on dry land.

Oceanic lithosphere
Mantle peridotite & serpentinite

THE ROCKS OF THE OCEAN CRUST come from the same source – mantle peridotite (*per-rid-o-tite*). This makes up the great volume of the Earth to about 400 kilometres down. It's made up of green minerals like olivine and pyroxene that are stable at the very high temperatures and pressures there – imagine 100 kilometres of rock sitting on your head at 1,200°C. At an ocean ridge where the two plates are slowly moving apart, mantle peridotite is able to rise. As it rises the pressure, due to the weight of the overlying rock, decreases and some of the peridotite melts to form a magma. This magma travels to within a few kilometres of the ocean floor where it can start to crystallise in a magma chamber into gabbro, be injected into fractures as a dolerite dyke, or be erupted at the ocean floor as a basalt lava. Together, these three rock types form most of the ocean crust. Their boundary with the underlying mantle is known as the **Moho** (Mohorovičić discontinuity) and is typically located about 7–10 kilometres below the ocean floor. We know this because seismic waves from earthquakes increase velocity as they pass from the lower density crustal rocks into the higher density mantle peridotite. At **Coverack Cove** you can actually stand on the Moho and see some of these transitions with your

Weathered rind on an outcrop of serpentinite south of Coverack.

own eyes. Here, within 300 metres you can walk from the dark green peridotite of the mantle (south end of Mill Beach) to a depleted peridotite (where minerals have started to melt out) to all sorts of transitional varieties and colours of gabbro (below Brenda's General Stores). It's not often Mother Earth lifts her skirt so you can glimpse her petticoats, but on the Lizard that's exactly what she does.

Serpentine – altered mantle peridotite

Oceanic mantle peridotite is rarely seen at the surface because most is returned to the deep mantle in subduction zones as oceans close and are destroyed. It's a particularly tough rock, having been forged deep inside the Earth but surprisingly, it's not the rough passage from the mantle that does the most to alter the peridotite, it's water. If Kryptonite makes Superman's knees go wobbly, then water does the same for peridotite. When it encounters seawater or groundwater a strong chemical reaction follows, raising the temperature of

Weathered (red) serpentinite from Kennack Sands.

the rock and increasing its volume by as much as half. The green minerals are converted to deep rich shades of red and yellow to make the mineral **serpentine** and rocks called **serpentinites** – the rocks for which the Lizard is famous. This process started as soon as is the peridotite encountered seawater 380 million years ago and is still happening with groundwater now. It explains why serpentinite, despite being such a tough rock, is such a poor building stone – exposed to rain, it simply expands and cracks. Out on the downs and cliffs the natural serpentinite outcrops are covered with a deeply fissured rind where the rock has expanded (*left*). It has a reddish appearance because serpentine is basically magnesium iron silicate and the iron part oxidises like rust. To the modern eye the deep rich colours of polished serpentine can be a bit garish, but the Victorians loved it and an industry grew up to supply columns and mantelpieces for London mansions and banks. A few craftsmen still work in **Lizard Town** and at **Lizard Point** making ornaments.

Serpentinised peridotite at Kennack Sands.

Oceanic lithosphere
Rocks of the oceanic crust

T HE STUFF THAT MELTS OUT of the mantle peridotite below the Moho is, broadly speaking, basalt magma. Which rock it eventually solidifies into has a lot to do with how quickly it cools. The first crystals to form (this takes tens, if not hundreds of years) fall like snowflakes to the base of the magma chamber near the Moho. Here they accumulate in drifts and eventually solidify into a rock called *troctolite* or *trout stone* made up of olivine and plagioclase. A red variety can be seen at **Mill Beach** in **Coverack** and a greener one at nearby **Perprean Cove**. Similar *cumulate rocks* outcrop in a broad arc around the serpentine of **Goonhilly Downs** but they're not very well exposed and have been metamorphosed into schists.

Troctolite from Coverack

Magma that cools slowly in the main part of the chamber forms a coarse-grained igneous rock called *gabbro*. This has a lovely

Gabbro

greyish-green hue, due to olivine and pyroxene crystallised from the melt. Great boulders sit on the surface at **Lowland Point**, **Crousa Downs** and **Main Dale**. At **Coverack** there are beautiful transitional varieties – including a handsome black variety with a bronze lustre. As the gabbro in the magma chamber starts to cool and solidify, minor earthquakes fracture the rock and basalt is injected into the fissures where it rapidly chills. These are the fine grained 'black dykes' seen at **Dean Quarry** and **Godrevy Cove** and they form the upper part of the crust close to the ocean floor. Some lava is squirted out like toothpaste directly onto the sea floor, building up layers several kilometres thick. They form pillow-like structures on the seabed. **Mullion Island** is a raft of pillow lava. Boat trips often get close enough to the cliffs for the pillow shapes to be clearly visible. A steady rain of ash and other deep sea sediments settle above and between the pillow lava completing the ophiolite sequence.

Transitional varieties of gabbro from the Moho boundary at Coverack.

Basalt dyke at Godrevy. Minor earthquakes fracture the gabbro & basalt is injected into the fissures.

Basalt lava erupted onto the sea floor is squirted out like toothpaste forming pillow shapes. Sediment collects on the ocean floor above.

Metamorphism & deformation

A SCHIST IS A ROCK OF ANY ORIGIN that has been deformed at high temperature and pressure so that it becomes stretched and is 'foliated'. As a consequence of earth movements the rock partially recrystallises, often into layers of different composition and colour. On the Lizard, all the rocks of the ophiolite – peridotite, gabbro, basalt, and ocean sediments – have been subjected to these forces and most, at least locally, are transformed to schists. A process known as *metamorphism* by geologists. Although the appearance of the rock can change greatly, its chemical composition remains essentially unaltered so that modern analysis can often reveal its origin. On the west coast of the Lizard you can see this characteristic layering in the serpentine. It's perhaps most striking in the in the blue/grey *Traboe Schists* of **Porthallow**, **Porthkerris** and **Mullion Cove**. These were once cumulate rocks (like troctolite) and gabbro. They look very different to the less deformed gabbro boulders on **Main Dale** and **Crousa Downs** near Coverack but they are the same rock just subjected to greater metamorphism and deformation. Similar looking schists occur at **Landewednack** and **Housel Bay**. Analysis has shown they were once pillow lava from the sea floor. At **Pystyll Ogo**, **Old Lizard Head** and south of **Porthallow** a misty brown rock called *Old Lizard Head Schist* was, 500 million years ago, mud and sandy sediment on the bottom of the sea.

The characteristic foliated or layered appearance of schist (altered gabbro) at Mullion Cove.

Old Lizard Head schist

Slates & sandstones near Loe Bar buckled by earth movements.

Man O'War & Kennack gneisses

A *gneiss* (pronounced *nice*) is a rock that has suffered even greater levels of metamorphism than a schist. The *Man O'War Gneiss* is a 500 million year old remnant of the Gondwanian continental plate that pushed north overriding the oceanic lithosphere of the Rheic Ocean. They were originally granites. The Man O'War Gneiss just makes it onto the southern tip of the Lizard at **Old Lizard Head** and on the **Man O'War Reef**. Blocks of it lie on the beach at **Pystyll Ogo**; it has a rather dreamy, corrugated appearance.

Kennack Gneiss is the distinctive pink rock you find on all the beaches on the east coast between **Kennack Sands** and **Landewednack**. This rock formed when the, still hot, block of Lizard ophiolite was being thrust upwards. The surrounding continental rocks melted and mingled with basalt magma. It's closely associated with the serpentine but is a much softer rock, forming the valleys at **Poltesco**, **Cadgwith** and **Gwendreath**.

Man O'War Gneiss

Serpentinite at Kennack Sands

Kennack Gneiss

The Kennack Gneiss extends inland to Goonhilly Downs but is very noticeably more fertile than the surrounding serpentine. It even supports woodland in great contrast to the shallow treeless valleys on serpentine, like **Downas Cove** and **Gew-graze**.

Roseland Breccia & Conglomerate

As the Gondwanian Plate drove north it acted like a giant bulldozer scraping and uplifting everything in its path, including sections of its own continental rocks that fell off the front edge as it advanced. Great rafts of pillow lava and quartzites – some hundreds of metres wide – are mixed together with limestones and slates to form a huge jumble. It makes up much of the good farming land of the Meneage. Conglomerate is a related rock found on the beach at **Men-aver** and **Gillan**. (*photo p58*) It's an underwater mix of small rocks and boulders that once filled a submarine canyon near the advancing front edge of Gondwana.

What can you see today?

Just from looking at the colourful pebbles on Lizard beaches a story has unfolded of how the Lizard was once oceanic lithosphere at the bottom of the Rheic Ocean. Of how that slice of ocean floor was trapped in a vice between two continents and how those rocks became deformed and metamorphosed. What is there to see of the larger structures of the ophiolite – the signature in stone that solved the puzzle of the Lizard rocks?

The slice of ophiolite on the Lizard is thin; it's no more 1 kilometre thick. It's made up of two or three sheets twisted and tilted against each other and showing different degrees of deformation. The classic ophiolite sequence is clearest in the Crousa Sheet where it has been tilted gently northwards so that as you walk the coast northwards you're also taking a journey from the mantle to the ocean floor. Between **Black Head** and **Coverack** you are walking over deep mantle rocks (serpentinised peridotite) from 10 kilometres down. The Moho boundary is at **Mill Beach** in **Coverack** and above that is the gabbro of **Lowland Point**, which ends with swarms of basalt dykes at **Godrevy** and **Manacle Point**. The topmost part of the sequence – pillow lava and ocean sediments – are missing or hidden under the sea. In this sheet the gabbro has been partially metamorphosed but it's never as severely deformed or recrystallised as the neighbouring Traboe Schist (*photo bottom left p16*) and it retains much of its crystalline appearance (*photo bottom left p14*).

The Goonhilly sheet seems to be a central dome of serpentine surrounded on three sides by schists – rocks that were once cumulates, gabbros and basalts but which have been deformed to the blue and white layered rocks of **Mullion Cove**, **Porthallow**, **Porthkerris** and **Porthoustock**.

The Man O'War sheet has some oceanic rocks, like the Landewednack schists (once pillow lavas) and some continental rocks like the Man O'War Gneiss (once granites) but they are older rocks that predate the creation of the Rheic Ocean.

A Blackthorn sloe ready to pick (about 1cm wide).
Along with Grey Willow, Blackthorn fills the more
sheltered valleys and cliff slopes & creates the
closest thing to woodland on the more exposed

Plants of the Lizard
An inadvertent Eden

I RECENTLY SAW THE BARELY CLAD BOTTOM of a naturalist sticking out of a small stream near Kynance. The only things he had on, besides his skimpy trunks, were a snorkel and mask. His head was underwater – no doubt searching for some rare plant or animal. You should expect to encounter this sort of behaviour on the Lizard – the sudden gleeful yelps as botanists and lichen hunters stumble across rarities. The Reverend Charles Johns, who in 1848 wrote one of the first guidebooks about the Lizard, laid his hat on the ground at **Caerthillian Valley** and covered three different species of clover – two found nowhere else in Britain. Famously in the world of lichens, five species new to the UK were discovered on a single morning in 1986. No wonder so many botanists are held spellbound on the Lizard.

There are more than 600 species of flowering plants on the Lizard, nearly a quarter of all UK species. It's all the more extraordinary when you consider that half of the Lizard is underlain by serpentine, a spectacularly barren, almost toxic bedrock that usually produces a sparse and specialist flora. The explanation for this paradoxical richness is found in part in the many different and unusual Lizard rocks. But above all, it seems to be a serendipitous coming together of multiple factors: a very mild maritime climate, but one prone to gales and salt winds; waterlogged and boggy soils, but ones that often parch and dry out in the summer; soils of greatly contrasting fertility and pH; and lastly man's influence, because the Lizard is far from the wild place it first appears. Any single factor taken on its own would have an interesting effect on the flora; taken together, they combine, overlap and interact in fascinating and surprising ways. Contrasting plant communities grow side-by-side in a mosaic that changes within a few metres but also changes markedly over time with the cycle of heath fires. It's not so much that conditions are ideal for growth, but that there is such a variety of different, difficult conditions. Each habitat, with its own combination of factors, attracts its own specialist plants.

Gorse & the pink threads of the parasitic plant Dodder. You can see the tender new growth which, for a few weeks in the spring, or after a heathland fire, is soft enough to be grazed by cattle.

Devil's-bit Scabious a plant of damp corner The devil irritated by its power to heal bit i root off.

Lousewort a semi-parasite that supplem its diet by sucking sap from nearby grasses.

Bell Heather

Cross-leaved Heather sometimes known in Cornwall as She-heath. Perhaps the most beautiful of the heather family with its downy grey green leaves. Found in the wetter parts of the downs.

Ling or Heather

Acid-loving flora

The influence of soil & bedrock

THE LIZARD HAS A GREAT VARIETY OF SOILS because it has a great variety of different rocks. Each soil has its own peculiarities that affect the flora. The most distinctive are the serpentine soils. As we've seen, serpentine is really a creature of the Earth's deep interior, and as if to make a point of its reluctant appearance at the surface, left to itself it forms a particularly sullen, unwilling and barren soil with few of the nutrients, like nitrogen, phosphorus and calcium, that plants need for growth. If that wasn't enough, it's also heavily laced with metals like magnesium, chromium and nickel which many plants find toxic. So it's no surprise that serpentine is closely associated with the areas of uncultivated heathland.

In the few places in the world where serpentine occurs on dry land it usually has a sparse and specialist flora. Essentially, plant life is a bit nonplussed when faced with the odd ingredients that make up serpentine. Those that do prosper have strategies that allow them to deal with its peculiarities. For instance, many plants cope with the low nutrient levels by simply being small and slow growing; serpentine soils rarely support anything as nutrient hungry as a tree. Some like *Dodder* and *Broomrape* have parasitic lifestyles that free them from the soil – they get their nutrients directly from their host. Others, like the insectivorous *Pale Butterwort*, supplement the meagre nutrition available by catching insects on their sticky leaves and brewing a nutritious fly soup. Even so, the Lizard is atypical of most serpentine areas because, far from having a limited flora, it's actually something of a botanical wonderland.

One example of this is that you'd expect to see a base-loving flora on serpentine because it's an ultra-basic rock. Instead, on many parts of the downs you come across a familiar cast of characters from the acid soils of Cornish cliff and

Tormentil

Cornish or Goonhilly Heath with its exuberant flower spikes. It dominates where the serpentine & gabbro bedrocks are expressed on the surface. The pink threads of the parasitic plant Dodder are embracing this plant and will feed on the sap for the rest of the summer.

Saw-wort

Bloody Cranesbill

Betony or the Devil's Plaything – a remedy for elf sickness.

Black Bog Rush dominates in the wetter areas – wherever you see this you know the walking will be difficult.

Dropwort above Kynance Cove – it prefers the drier base-rich soils of the downs.

Base-loving flor

moor: the demur pink-flowered *Ling* or *Heather*; the deep purple flowers of *Bell Heather*; in damper corners the glamorous *Cross-leaved Heath* and the sweet coconut scented *Gorse*. Between them you'll find *Lousewort*, *Tormentil* and *Devils-bit*. This is odd because base-loving and acid-loving floras have contrasting and mutually exclusive biochemical needs. Acid-loving plants cannot thrive on base soils and vice versa, but on the Lizard they are frequently found growing side-by-side. The explanation lies in the soil's origin. In many places on the Lizard the soil has been imposed from above rather than deriving from the bedrock below. Here the influence of the base-rich serpentine and gabbro is masked by layers of acidic peat and loess – a wind-blown silt that covered Europe during glacial periods. Where serpentine emerges at the surface; where peat and loess have been eroded away on valley slopes; where man has dug a quarry, a ditch or a prehistoric barrow or where the peat and soil have been removed for fuel, then the base-loving flora proclaims itself. This is most clearly signalled by the appearance of the free-flowering *Cornish Heath*. Unusually for the heather family this is one member that loves, and is confined to, base-rich soils.

The very high levels of magnesium in serpentine, as much as 2,000 times more than in a granite soil, seem to be a particular problem for many plants, although some coastal species like *Thrift* and *Scurvy Grass* seem at home here. After a fire on the downs, they often turn up along with drifts of *Oxeye Daisy* much further inland than you would normally expect. It's possible they've evolved strategies for dealing with the much lower concentrations of magnesium in the salt-drenched soils of the coast. Added to that, the very infertility of the serpentine soil protects them from being crowded out, as they usually are on more 'normal' soils, by more vigorous inland species.

The influence of serpentine bedrock is often masked by deposits of acidic loess – a fine silt blown across Europe during glacial periods.

Self-heal

Red Clover

White Clover

A heath fire on Main Dale near Coverack gives Slender St Johns Wort a chance to bloom before the charred stem of Cornish Heath regenerates.

Sheep's-bit Scabious – common on dry stony banks & hedges.

Heath Spotted Orchid – found on Crousa Downs & Main Dale near Coverack & on the cliffs at Mullion Cove.

Gabbro & Schist

Gabbro & schist soils

In one of those eye-catching contrasts so typical of the Lizard, the gabbro can, where it's deeply rotted and weathered, form remarkably fertile soils the texture and colour of velvety cocoa. The fields south of **St Keverne** and **Roskilly's** produce thick crops of wheat and barley. The contrast between serpentine soils and those of the weathered gabbro is best seen at **Gwenter** behind **Kennack Sands**. A small stream follows the line of a fault between the Crousa and Goonhilly sheets of ophiolite so there isn't the usual gradual transition between the rocks here. To the west is the uncultivated serpentine heathland of Goonhilly Downs; to the east on the gabbro are the farms of **Trelan** and **Gwenter**. Sit on one of the barrows overlooking this little valley and you can see at a glance, just from the vegetation, where the serpentine ends and the gabbro begins. It's a very striking moment – one that gives you an insight into the large-scale processes at work in this landscape.

On **Crousa Downs** and **Main Dale** large blocks of gabbro, called *crusairs*, weather out and sit above the surface and the gabbro is only lightly rotted. Here you find a variation in the heath flora of the serpentine and between the *Cornish Heath*, you find *Slender St John's Wort* with *Heath Spotted*, *Lesser Butterfly* and *Fragrant* orchids.

The soils formed above schist (recrystallised gabbro and basalt) are mostly free of the difficulties associated with serpentine and so are generally fertile and farmed. Around Lizard Town they are particularly freely draining, and in the summer this often induces drought conditions that mimic a Mediterranean climate. The south-facing slopes of **Caerthillian Valley** are famous for their clovers including *Long-headed*, *Upright*, *Bird's Foot*, *Suffocated* (the flower is lost beneath the sward), *Twin Headed* and *Zigzag* among others.

Spring Sandwort, a plant that has evolved a taste for metal-rich soils. Found only on the Lizard & the waste tips of lead mines in the Mendips.

Bog Asphodel on Goonhilly

Hemlock Water Dropwort at Lowland Point – beautiful but deadly.

Meadowsweet above Kynance Cove it loves damp corner & ditches.

Greater Horsetail in the valley below Roskilly's.

Flag Iris at Lowland Point

Wet & boggy

Hemp Agrimony – common in damp roadside ditches.

The influence of climate & exposure

THE CHEMISTRY OF THE SOILS AND BEDROCK are primary influences on the flora but there are other important influences that straddle the geological boundaries – in particular, the impact of climate and exposure. The climate here is deeply influenced by the surrounding sea; it's warm, moist and almost frost free. In fact it's so mild that the Lizard is a far northern outpost for Lusitanian plants like *Cornish Heath*, *Pale Butter-wort* and *Fringed Rupture-wort* – species that really belong on the Atlantic coasts of Portugal, Spain and France. Escapees from local gardens cloak the cliffs at **Lizard Point** and **Coverack** – Southern African plants like *Hottentot Fig* and *Mesembryanthemum*. Even sub-tropical plants like *Agave* and *Gunnera* grow happily in the gardens at **Trebah**, **Carwinion**, **Bosahan** and **Glendurgan**. You can find tadpoles in the deep track ruts at **Croft Pascoe Forest** at Christmas while other parts of the UK are covered in snow and ice.

Wet & boggy

Serpentine weathers to a claggy, impervious yellow clay that impedes drainage. After rain the downs can be like a lake with water standing, often for weeks and sometimes months, in pools, track ruts and in the runnels between tussocks of *Purple Moor Grass*. This is aggravated by the absence of a clear pattern of drainage. Millions of years of rain and wind have made little impact on the serpentine and it retains a flat seabed profile from when it was planed flat by waves. This is particularly obvious at **Vellan Head** (*photo p95*). Deposits of sea pebbles on **Crousa Downs** from this time are now 100 metres above today's sea level.

Ragged Robin at Lowland Point.

The wettest areas are revealed by the presence of *Black Bog Rush* and large tussocks of soft rustling *Purple Moor Grass* – areas which you soon learn to avoid as you walk the downs.

Sea Mayweed

Sea Campion

Bird's Foot Trefoil
above Kynance

Common Centaury

Spring Squill – first to flower on the cliff.
It has a late flowering cousin – Autumn Squill.

Grassy Cliff

Kidney Vetch
(Bacon & Eggs)

The damp runnels between the tussocks have a little ecosystem all of their own with *Bog Pimpernel, Creeping Willow and Land Quillwort. Great Burnet* (*photo p4*) survives prolonged periods of flooding by retreating to its thick underground stems (rhizomes) and can be found happily growing in the waterlogged conditions on the highest point of the downs at **Dry Tree** along with crowds of spiky yellow *Bog Asphodel*. The high rainfall and lack of drainage promote the acidic conditions needed for the formation of peat. It takes only a few centimetres to form a pocket large enough for acid-loving heathers to get established. This explains the curious phenomenon of base and acid-loving plants growing so close together. Wherever relief can be found from the boggy conditions – on hedges, walls, prehistoric barrows, even the little mounds that used to hold anti-glider poles – *Bell Heather* and *Gorse* are noticeably heathier. In boggy areas *Heather* keeps its feet dry by growing into the tussocks of *Purple Moor Grass*.

The Lizard gets a little less rain in the summer than many other areas of Cornwall because it's low lying. The thin soils over the serpentine, gabbro and the free-draining schist struggle to retain water in the summer and are soon parched, mimicking a Mediterranean climate. Some plants like the tiny *Land Quillwort* have adapted to this by having their growing season in the winter and by becoming dormant in the summer. Animals and plants rush to complete their life cycles before the summer drought.

On the cliffs

In general, the difficulties of living on the exposed coast with its drying winds, burning salt spray and meagre soils, trump the influence of any particular bedrock and it's a place were coastal specialists dominate. Anything that pokes its head up risks getting it blown off, so this is no place for delicate leaves and flowers. To survive here you need to be tough. Prostrate (low-growing) forms like *Prostrate Asparagus* on **Asparagus Island** and the *Juniper* bushes at **Gew-graze** are common. In places the *Heather* and *Gorse* are pruned by the wind so they are only 10cm

The cliff face – a mix of Thrift & Rock Samphire on the dark blue schist cliffs at Mullion Cove. The orange lichen has the beautiful name of Xanthoria.

Rock Sea-spurrey

Fringed Rupture-wo

Rock Samphire in flower on the lowest parts of exposed cliffs at Polurrian. Its long woody roots penetrate deep into bare rock crevices in the spray. The variety found in the west has particularly fleshy thick triangular leaves. *Samphire* comes from *St Pierre* – the herb of St Peter the fisherman. He is the rock of the church and Samphire grows out of the bare rock.

Hottentot Fig

English Stonecrop

Exposed Cliff

high. They hug the ground where the wind is slower and where cover reduces drying out of the soil. The heathland flora alters subtly as it approaches the coast at **Predannack** and **Lizard Downs**. *Cornish Heath* and *Gorse* become less frequent and *Heather* dominates. This is probably one of the few truly natural habitats on the Lizard.

Gathering and retaining water is one of the great challenges in this environment. Many plants have small, waxy fleshy leaves to store water and reduce water loss. On the lowest parts of exposed cliffs well within reach of the spray from waves is *Rock Samphire*. Its long woody roots penetrate deep into bare rock crevices. A little higher up the cliff *Thrift* and *Rock Sea-spurrey* perform a similar feat. On the rocky outcrops *English Stonecrop* with its tiny succulent leaves seems to exist on bare rock alone.

In the summer, the grassy cliffs like **Pen Olver**, **Kynance Heights** and **Lizard Head** and the sheltered slopes of headlands like **Chynhalls** and **Lankidden**, put on one of the most colourful shows on the coast. One of the first flowers to appear in early spring is the adorable *Spring Squill*, dusting the cliffs in blue sparkles. *Sea Campion* forms great drifts on the sunny side of field walls along with *Kidney Vetch*, *Rest Harrow*, *Sea Carrot* and *Bird's-foot Trefoil*. Later in the summer, the small pink flowers of *Common Centaury* are accompanied by *Wild Thyme* and *Sheep's-bit Scabious* particularly on the schists of **Housel Bay** and **Lizard Point**. On **Kynance Heights** *Thyme Broomrape* takes all the nutrients it needs from the roots of *Wild Thyme*, sending up a stubby red flower stalk in early to mid-summer (*photo p92*). It's not the only parasitic plant on the coast. *Gorse* and *Heath* are often covered in the tangled pink and red threads of *Dodder*.

Honeysuckle

Kynance North Valley. Paths criss-cross the downs behind Kynance & Predannack.

The influence of humans

THE DOWNS THAT FEEL SO WILD ARE, to a large degree, a product of man's activities. From the first moment he set foot here he has cut, burned and cleared. He has stripped away the peat and soil for fuel, unmasking the full influence of the serpentine bedrock on the flora. More recently, quarrying has created numerous pools and ponds that teem with amphibians and insects. Even the Luftwaffe joined in, adding a few bomb craters on Goonhilly in 1941. And a little surprisingly, at a time where man's influence on the environment is often portrayed as malign, the effect has been to increase the richness of wildlife, creating an inadvertent Eden.

A dynamic and unstable environment

The most recent glacial period reached its peak about 20,000 years ago. Enormous ice sheets reached as far south as the Bristol Channel and the Lizard was a sub-arctic landscape of grassland, *Birch*, *Scots Pine* and *Juniper* (a few bushes still cling on at **Gew-graze Valley**). Humans, who had reached Britain in previous warm periods, had long retreated to warmer refuges in southern Europe. When the thaw came, about 13,000 years ago, they started to move up from Iberia to Brittany and across to Cornwall. So much water was still locked up in the northern ice sheets that it's possible they walked across what is now the bed of the English Channel to get here. They carried with them, on their clothes and belongings, spores and seeds of plants from their Lusitanian home, species like *Cornish Heath* and *Fringed Rupture-wort*. A rapid rise in sea levels 6,000 years ago stranded these Lusitanian plants far from their homeland.

When the first prehistoric people arrived here it seems unlikely that the downs or the more exposed parts of the west coast were ever thickly wooded because the soils are just too poor and the exposure just too great. The camps of the first (Mesolithic) people seem to be mostly on these naturally open areas. Hazel nut fragments, a favourite prehistoric food, unearthed at a coastal settlement at **Poldowrian** have been

Prehistoric flint blade

radiocarbon dated to around 7,500 years ago. As farming became established the downs seem to have been intensively grazed, encouraging the growth of grasses and holding in check natural regeneration. In the Bronze Age (2000BC–800BC) barrows were being built on top of grassland at **Goonhilly**. A combination of nutrient loss and heavier rainfall seems to have led to an increase in the formation of peat about 3,000 years ago favouring the acid-loving flora. As the cliffs and lower slopes of the high ground were progressively cleared for cultivation, grazing on the downs seems to have become less intense allowing the development of the sort of heathland we see today. Heath will readily burn and then, as now, burning was used to promote soft growth for cattle to graze. It also resets the biological clock so the habitat is kept in a state of perpetual adolescence. The canopy of heather and gorse is burnt away and, at least for a few years, *Foxglove*, *Oxeye Daisy* and thistles carpet the blackened downs as *Cornish Heath* and *Gorse* regenerate from their charred stumps. Pollen evidence seems to suggest that in prehistory *Cornish Heath* was not the dominant plant of the downs that it is today. Widespread cutting of peat in the C14th and C15th to fuel the smelting of tin pared away the masking effect of the loess and peat to reveal the full effect of the base-rich bedrock. It's at this time that the base-loving flora and, in particular, *Cornish Heath* seems to have become dominant.

Ponds, bomb craters, quarries & cart tracks

In addition to the more-or-less permanent pools at **Hayle Kimbo**, **Croft Pascoe** and **Ruan's Pool** (which may well have been dug by prehistoric man), the downs are covered by numerous ephemeral pools and a patchwork of micro-habitats in cart tracks, bomb craters and small quarry pits. Here in the spring and early summer before the pools dry out, *Pillwort*, *Water-crowfoot*, *Chives* and *Yellow Centaury* bloom. The pools are full of invertebrate and amphibian larvae.

A story told in pebbles & plants

I HOPE THAT GALLOP THROUGH the geology and flora of the Lizard goes some way to explaining why this corner of West Cornwall excites so much interest and ardour. On the Lizard a colourful pebble or a rare flower unlocks a much bigger story. A serpentine pebble at **Kynance** is a postcard from the Earth's deep interior, a memento of the doomed Rheic Ocean. After a swim at **Jangye-ryn**, take a moment to examine the contorted strata in the low cliffs behind the beach – they tell a story of a restless Earth where oceans, mountains and continents are perpetually created and destroyed.

It's been nearly 50 years since plate tectonics finally solved the puzzle of these unusual rocks and unravelled the story of their birth. Even so it's difficult to comprehend the forces that could pick up a block of oceanic floor 15 miles wide and thrust it onto a Cornish shore. On the Lizard as you walk across the cliffs from Godrevy to Lowland Point and Coverack you're also making a journey *in* to the Earth. From the pillow lavas of the Rheic Ocean seabed to the grey-green crystals of gabbro in the magma chamber to the mantle rocks south of Coverack, you are walking across a story as well as a landscape.

For botanists too, the Lizard is full of surprising moments. The very particular and unusual circumstances on the Lizard – its variety of rocks and soils; its exposure and climate; its various and diverse habitats – show how plants improvise and adapt. It's striking how many plants appear in slightly odd situations and in odd combinations as if they've been thrown together on some sort of seaside vacation. Where else can you step from a Mediterranean flora to that of the moors of Northern Europe or in the space of a few metres move from the serpentine flora of La Coruña and the Massif Central to a flora more reminiscent of the chalk downs of Dorset?

The thickly wooded banks of the Helford have hardly changed since the first Mesolithic hunters walked here 6,000 years ago. This is Gweek, at the head of the estuary, on the path to Pemboa.

1. Helford & The Meneage
Gweek, Helford Village to St Keverne & Coverack

I N THIS BOOK, we're mainly concerned with the southern bank of the Helford – an area known as **The Meneage**. The north bank is covered by our *Falmouth & Roseland Guidebook*. This is a very rural area, heavily wooded and cultivated since at least the Iron Age (800BC–AD43). It's a landscape typical of slate – gently rolling countryside, low cliffs and wooded creeks. The tidal creeks have a secretive and conspiratorial atmosphere best experienced at **Tremayne Quay** and **Frenchman's Creek**. They appear quite forlorn when the tide is out.

Helford Village and **Helford Passage** on the opposite bank are the only places on the river that you might describe as 'busy' and even then, it's only really in the summer holidays when the river fills with yachts. The only other place of any size is **Gweek** at the head of the river. Getting around the Helford by car is not that easy. The road network holds the river in a slightly awkward embrace, either clinging uncomfortably to the riverbank, or madly ascending and descending the steep valley sides. The maze of small lanes give only brief glimpses of the river and perhaps the most pleasurable way to see the river is to pack a picnic, hire a motor boat and chug upriver calling at one of the small quays like **Tremayne** or Scott's Quay.

In Cornish, *Meneage* translates as '*the land of monasteries*'. Here in the C5th and C6th, just as on the nearby River Fal, Celtic holy men and women set up sanctuaries on the river banks and in the wooded valleys. Many grew into small communities and 600 years after their foundation, into the churches we see today at **Manaccan**, **St Keverne** and **St Anthony**. At **Merther Uny**, above **Gweek** there is a rare survival – an early site that has remained as it was 1,000 years ago.

GETTING ABOUT
BY FERRY
In the summer, an 'on-demand' foot ferry connects **Helford Village** to **Helford Passage**. From here you can easily walk to the gardens at Trebah & Glendurgan. Bikes OK. A smaller ferry connects **St Anthony** to the other side of **Gillan Creek** saving a long walk round.

Ferry pontoon at Helford Passage

BY CAR
The network of small lanes around the Meneage can be a little disorientating – expect to have to do quite a bit of reversing.

BY BUS
Gweek & the famous gardens on the north bank (Trebah, Glendurgan & Carwinion) are served by Helston - Gweek - Falmouth bus (35).

BOAT HIRE
At Helford Passage & St Anthony – see Helpful Info

Walk 1

Gweek & Merther Uny

At the tide's limit

Helston
Gweek

Lizard Point

BUS

Helston - Falmouth bus via Gweek, jump off at the Gweek stop for the southern part of this walk or, take the Falmouth - Helston bus via the main road (A394) for the northern part of this walk, Trevenen stop. For a longer, one-way walk, jump off at Laity, walk to Seworgan & then follow the stream south to Merther Uny & pick up the bus at Gweek to return to Helston.

PARKING

Very limited in this area. Parking in Gweek during the summer can be tricky. There's some roadside parking at Boskenwyn.

FOOD & DRINK

Gweek & Constantine (1.5km east of Merther Uny) both have a shop & pub. Cafe at The Grange Fruit Farm.

LOOK OUT FOR...

- Tolvan Stone & Merther Uny Round
- The Grange Fruit Farm
- Seal Sanctuary at Gweek

We try to include at least one walk in every book that's off the tourist trail and in Cornwall that often means an inland walk. At Gweek, paths fan out from the head of the estuary, west along a broad valley to **Mellangoose** and **Pemboa,** and north towards the granite uplands of Carnmenellis. In the valleys around **Seworgan** signs of tin mining are everywhere – derelict waterwheels, old chimneys and engine houses. The valley floors have all been turned over in search of stream tin, a naturally graded tin ore washed from the granite bedrock. This area has two of the best, but least known, prehistoric sites in Cornwall. At **Tolvan Cross** there's a prehistoric holed stone and at **Merther Uny** an Iron Age fortified farmstead known as a 'round' which was later reused as an early Christian sanctuary.

Gweek

The Seal Sanctuary brings visitors in the summer but essentially Gweek is a working harbour and has been for at least 2,000 years. In prehistory, the main trading port on the Helford seems to have been further down the river at **Gear Camp** near **Trelowarren**. It probably moved to Gweek during the Romano-British period (AD43–AD410) as the old order was overturned. Large quantities of Roman pottery fragments have been found around the harbour, which led a quiet existence for 800 years or so until Helston's harbour on the River Cober became choked by the shingle of Loe Bar. Then Gweek became the port for Helston, taking on a lucrative trade from local tin mines that only ended 120 years ago. The last great sailing ships that docked in Gweek called here to carry miners and their families to Australia and America in the great emigration that followed the closure of the mines.

The boat yard at Gweek

Tolvan stone

One of the least known but most impressive
standing stones in Cornwall is in the back garden
of the house at Tolvan Cross and you'll need to
knock and ask to see it. Usually these prehistoric
stones, which are about 4,000 years old, are simply
upright blocks like **Dry Tree Menhir** on **Goonhilly**.
A very few, like the Mên-an-tol in
West Penwith, are holed but none are
as large as this, which has even had
sections cut away in the past to make
gateposts. The triangular shape recalls
a menhir at Boscawen-noon Farm
near Penzance. There are prehistoric
barrows in the surrounding fields and
you can see one just over the road in
the corner of the field – a low mound
now no more than half a metre high.

Above
An early (C10th?) granite cross stands within the *lann* or *sacred enclosure* of Merther Uny in its original position near the west entrance (now blocked). Just east & behind this cross are the graves of the Christian community that lived here. Crosses like this probably mark places where outdoor sermons were preached.

Below
Meruny cross in its original setting marking the way to the lann.

Merther Uny

If you're not into prehistory or the Dark Ages you're probably not going to get too excited by Merther Uny. But if you are, this is an outstanding site. You are standing looking at an early Christian sanctuary, at least 1,000 years old, which itself stands within an Iron Age *round* or fortified farmstead which is 1,000 years older still. Excavations in the 1960s revealed C1st BC to C2nd AD pottery and evidence of a timber stockade on the surrounding oval bank. Inside, it would have had all the functions of a farm: two or three thatched round house huts similar in style to those at **Kynance Gate**, stock pens, kennels, perhaps a small shrine, a workshop for toolmaking and possibly a small forge for smelting stream tin to be traded at **Gear Camp**.

Almost all rounds were abandoned in the C5th and C6th when, for reasons not fully understood, numerous settlements moved, often only a few hundred metres, to new sites nearby. Many are still recognisable, marooned in the landscape as oval fields. We've marked some on the maps but there isn't usually much to see. Sometime between the C6th and C10th the abandoned round at Merther Uny was reused as an early Christian *lann* or *sanctuary*. In Cornish *merther* means *saint's grave* and *Uny* is *St Euny* – a well-known West Cornwall saint. It was a small communal settlement with a wooden chapel, the granite cross that still stands today and a graveyard. At some point the chapel was rebuilt in stone, parts of which were later robbed and used in the nearby farm buildings when the site fell into disuse. The nearby churches at **Constantine** and **Mawnan** are also set in abandoned rounds. This site never developed beyond its early stages.

Merther Uny
Early Christian Sanctuary

Footpath to Seworgan 1.8km

Trevenen

Trussall

Treloquithack Farm

Trillian Farm

Treloquithack

Merther Uny Farm

Mertheruny Mill

Polanguy Farm

Meruny Cross

Mellanzea

Trevilges Farm

Tregoose Farm

Polglase Farm

Bufton

Polglase Wood

Melli

Granite Slate

Gweek Lane

Grambla Farm

Woodside Farm

Grambla British Fort

Tolvan

ergate

P **Boskenwyn**
School

Barton Farm

Tolvan Cross

Watergate Cottage

Na D

Boskenwyn Manor

Trenoweth Farm

Tolvan Stone
Bronze Age holed stone

Manor Cottage Farm

Candon Water Far

Pollard Farm

B o s k e n w y n   D o w n s

Lower Boskenwyn

Boskenwyn Prehistoric Barrow

Marne Farm

Tregoon Farm

Gweek Nursery

Gweek

G w e e k   D o w n s

Pollard Mill

Boat Yard

Lower Quay

Gweek Drive

boa

Mellangoose Stream

Trevilgan Farm

Iron Age Round

Ponson

Fernycombe

35

The Grange

Gwarth-an-drea Plantation

t Air Arm
ng area,
tours

Zelah Farm

Higher Trevilga

Walk 1
Merther Uny
- 11km (7 miles)
- 4–5 hours

| 0 | 0.25km | 0.5km | 0.75km | 1km |

| 0 | ¼ mile | | ½ mile | |

P Rose-in-the-bush

Gilly Gabben

Treverry Farm

Gwarth

Mawgan

Halliggye fogou.
An underground
passage associated
with an Iron Age
round or fortified
farmstead. Their
function is unknown
– suggestions range
from domestic
(a food store) to
defence or even
religious.

Trelowarren Woods & Halliggye Fogou

Woodland walks, hill forts & a fogou

Walk 2

Gweek

Trelowarren

Lizard Point

Trelowarren woodland walk & Halliggye fogou are only open from 1 Apr to 30 Sept

BUS
Helston - Coverack - St Keverne bus, Garras Methodist Church stop. It's a 2.2km (1¼ mile) walk from here to Trelowarren House but the walk is pleasant, following the drive past Halliggye fogou. You can also pick the bus up at Double Lodges.

CAR PARKS
Plenty of space to park at Trelowarren and there are 4 or 5 spaces next to Halliggye fogou.

FOOD & DRINKS
Ice cream, teas, lunch & dinner available at New Yard Restaurant, Trelowarren. Nearest pubs – Mawgan & Newtown. Spar Shop in Mawgan, farm shop at Gear.

LOOK OUT FOR...
- Halliggye Fogou (take a torch, closes in the bat breeding season)
- Woodland walk followed by tea & cake at Trelowarren

This attractive landscape, an alternating mix of fields and woodland, has probably changed little since the Iron Age (800BC–AD43). You can see that in the way many Iron Age rounds (fortified farms) have been incorporated into the pattern of fields. At **Halliggye** near **Trelowarren House** there's an example of a round with a fogou – a curious underground passage. At **Gear** there are the impressive earth ramparts of an Iron Age encampment. **Trelowarren House** isn't open to the public but the stables and outhouses are and have been converted into a bistro, gallery and craft shop. Between Easter and the end of September you can park near the house and wander down through the woods and link up with the walk to **Tremayne Quay** on the river.

Gear Camp & Caervallack

Gear's main period of activity was from about 400BC to AD100 but, as with many similar sites, its use seems to stretch back into the Stone Age. These large camps are now thought to be less about military might and more about trade and communal activity, establishing the sort of functions that would later develop in medieval towns – a place for trade, fairs and market days and where disputes could be settled and justice dispensed. Imagine a Roman ship gently slipping into Mawgan Creek, the traders disembarking to be greeted by locals and making their way through the woods to Gear to trade oil, pottery and exotic fruits like grapes and dates for tin collected from the local streams. The enclosure at **Caervallack** is much smaller and more domestic, possibly a residence for the local king or a manor house, a forerunner of Trelowarren. *Time Team* looked at both these sites in Series 9, Episode 7.

Above
Trelowarren House.
The house isn't open to
the public but the stables
& outhouses are & have
been converted into a
bistro, gallery & craft
shop.
Below
The New Yard Restaurant
at Trelowarren serves
meals, ice creams and
teas.

Halliggye Fogou

Fogous are stone-lined underground passages. *Ogo* is
Cornish for *cave*. They date from the Middle Iron Age
(C4th BC) and this is one of the finest in Cornwall. It's
nearly 40 metres long and unusually well constructed.
Their function is a complete mystery as few objects
have been found inside that might suggest a use.
They do recall the much earlier Bronze Age passage
graves of Scilly and West Cornwall, like Tregiffian
near Lamorna. A ceremonial or religious function
certainly suits the scale and quality of construction
but they don't have the formality of a tomb. There's no
surrounding kerb, or impressive siting in the landscape.
I'm not aware of human remains ever having been
found inside a fogou and also the burial fashion in the
Iron Age was to expose the body to animals and the
elements, allowing it to become defleshed.

Another suggestion is that fogous might be
collective food stores like a prehistoric walk-in cold
room, but you would have thought food would soon
perish in the damp conditions. One thing we do
know is that they always seem to be associated with
settlements. The fogou is often the only part of the
settlement that remains intact – too large and too
difficult to plough down.

Halliggye Farm sits within the original round and
the modern road follows the north eastern quadrant
of the defensive bank and ditch. There's a small creep
passage that opens from the fogou into the ditch. The
only more impressive example is at Carn Euny, west of
Penzance, which forms part of an excavated prehistoric
village so the fogou sits in a more complete context.
The last use of this fogou was as an ammunition dump
for the Home Guard in World War 2.

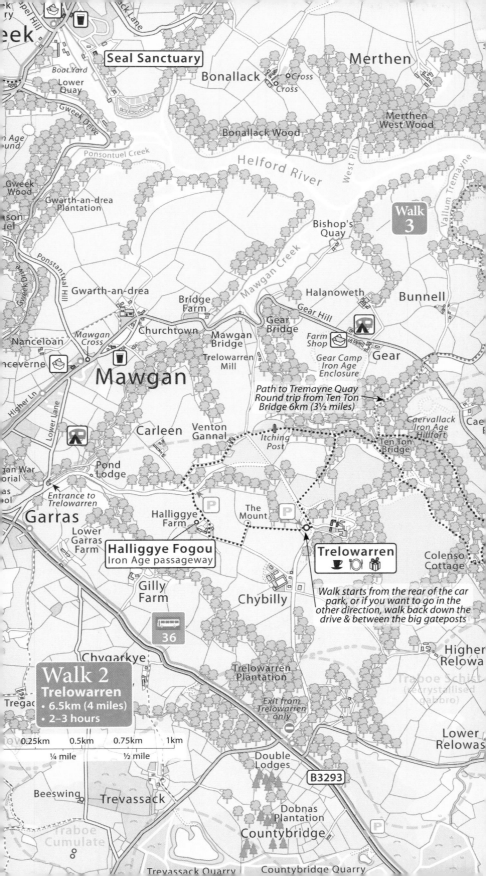

Seal Sanctuary

Merthen

Bonallack

Cross
Cross

Merthen
West Wood

Bonallack Wood

Boat Yard
Lower
Quay

Gweek Drive

Ponsontuel Creek

Helford River

West Pill

Gweek
Wood

Gwarth-an-drea
Plantation

Bishop's
Quay

Walk
3

Vallum Tremayne

Ponstantual Hill

Gwarth-an-drea

Bridge
Farm

Mawgan Creek

Halanoweth

Bunnell

Gear Hill

Gweek Drive

Nanceloan

Mawgan
Cross

Churchtown

Mawgan
Bridge

Gear
Bridge

Farm
Shop

Gear

nceverne

Mawgan

Trelowarren
Mill

Gear Camp
Iron Age
Enclosure

Caervallack
Iron Age
Hillfort

Cae

Higher Ln

Path to Tremayne Quay
Round trip from Ten Ton
Bridge 6km (3½ miles)

Lower Lane

Carleen

Venton
Gannal

Itching
Post

Ten Ton
Bridge

an War
orial

Pond
Lodge

P

The
Mount

P

s
ool

Entrance to
Trelowarren

Garras

Halliggye
Farm

Halliggye Fogou
Iron Age passageway

Trelowarren

Lower
Garras
Farm

Colenso
Cottage

Gilly
Farm

Chybilly

Walk starts from the rear of the car
park, or if you want to go in the
other direction, walk back down the
drive & between the big gateposts

36

Higher
Relowa

Chygarkye

Traboe Schis
(Crystallised
gabbro)

Walk 2
Trelowarren
• 6.5km (4 miles)
• 2–3 hours

Trelowarren
Plantation

Tregac

Exit from
Trelowarren
only

Lower
Relowas

0.25km   0.5km   0.75km   1km

¼ mile   ½ mile

Beeswing

Trevassack

Double
Lodges

B3293

P

aboe
umulate

Dobnas
Plantation

Countybridge

Trevassack Quarry   Countybridge Quarry

Walk 3

Tremayne Quay
Through the woods to the river

Gweek

Trelowarren

Lizard Point

BUS
Helston - St Keverne bus. Garras Methodist Church stop & then a 3.5km (2¼ mile) walk through Trelowarren Estate (open 1 Apr–30 Sept).

CAR PARKING
There are 2 or 3 roadside spaces in the valley at the start of this walk but because it's very popular, you can't count on them being free. Plenty of parking at Trelowarren House in the summer.

FOOD & DRINKS
Ice cream, teas, lunch & dinner available at Trelowarren New Yard Restaurant. Nearest pubs – Mawgan & Newtown. Spar Shop in Mawgan, farm shop at Gear.

LOOK OUT FOR...
- This walk is open all year but the Trelowarren woodland walk is only open 1 Apr–30 Sept.
- Arrive on a hired boat from Helford Passage
- Picnic on Tremayne Quay

This lovely walk follows the final part of the driveway that once connected **Trelowarren House** to the river at **Tremayne Quay**. It's a good walk for children; the track is easy going and there's plenty of room for a picnic on the quay itself. They will love exploring the banks of Vallum Tremayne Creek. The National Trust, who own the quay, allows boats to moor here, so arriving on a hired motor boat from Helford Passage or St Anthony is also an option. In the summer you can link up with the woodland walks around Trelowarren.

Great Wood and Merthen Wood have a documented history reaching back almost 1,000 years but they were ancient even then. Oak woodland first spread north from southern Europe as temperatures climbed at the end of the last glacial period 8,000 years ago. What we see here today isn't the wild wood that once reached up onto the downs, the wood that Stone Age man first encountered. As soon as people arrived they started to cut and manage the woodland, making glades to entice prey, cutting trees for coppice poles and harvesting hazel nuts, which were an important part of the Stone Age diet. By the Iron Age, about 3,000 years ago, most of the wild wood had been tamed. What remained probably very much resembled what we see now growing on the poor soils of the valley slopes. We think of ourselves as the great shapers of the landscape, but it was the prehistoric people with their stone axes who tamed the wild wood and had the greatest single impact on the landscape.

Arriving at Tremayne Quay after walking through the woods

Bonallack Wood

Merthen
West Wood

Merthen
Hole Quay

Tremayne
Quay

Helford River

West Pill

Middle Pill

Little
Wood

Vallum Tremayne

Great Wood

Tremayne

Bishop's
Quay

Trele

Mawgan Creek

Halanoweth

Bunnell

Mudgeo
Farm

Gear Hill

Gear
Bridge

Mudgeon
Vean

Mawgan
Bridge

Farm
Shop

Trelowarren
Mill

Gear Camp
Iron Age
Enclosure

Gear

P₂

Large stone blocks on
the roadside mark the
path to Trelowarren

Walk 3
Tremayne Quay
• 4km (2½ miles)
• 1–2 hours

Caervallack
Iron Age
Hillfort

Caervallack
Farm

nton
annal

Itching
Post

Ten Ton
Bridge

0   0.25km   0.5km   0.75km   1km

0   ¼ mile   ½ mile

Walk
2

P

The
Mount

P

Trecoose

Sch

St M

Walk 4

Frenchman's Creek, Kestle & Helford Village

Conspiratorial creeks (& amorous pirates)

Helford

Manaccan

Lizard Point

HELFORD FERRY
❶ An 'on-demand' pedestrian ferry service runs between Helford Passage & Helford Point from Easter to the end of October. Bikes permitted. ☎ (01326) 250770

BUS
There's no bus service on the Helford Village side. The (very) roundabout alternative is to catch the Helston - Gweek - Falmouth bus to the top of Helford Passage Hill on the north side of the river (1 hr journey). Walk down Passage Hill and cross the river by ferry. You'd deserve a medal for that.

CAR PARKING
Large car park at Helford Village & roadside parking for 5 beyond Kestle.

FOOD & DRINKS
Pubs & cafes in Helford Village & Manaccan. Helford Post Office & Manaccan Stores sell food & snacks.

LOOK OUT FOR...
• Kestle Barton Gallery

Frenchman's Creek is famously the setting for Daphne Du Maurier's romantic novel of a swashbuckling French pirate and his love affair with a passionate Cornish lady. Or, as the movie strap line puts it, *'In her elegant world ...a lady of ice: in his world of adventure ...a woman of fire!'* – an echo of the duality of the author's own life. The creek is very atmospheric especially early in the morning or the late evening, and like many woodland walks, it's enchanting in the rain. When the tide is out it has some of the eerie ambience of *Rebecca*. Daphne Du Maurier actually spent her honeymoon moored in the creek having sailed down from Fowey on her wedding day. Foy Vyvyan, who lived at Trelowarren, was a great friend and Du Maurier frequently went to stay. It's a bit difficult to imagine, given how quiet and tranquil the creek is now, that this was once a busy place with three quays serving the local farms. West Quay is used by local fishermen to store nets. Children love running around the woods and paths and there's an old derelict boat hidden away on a tiny beach below the path.

Frenchman's Creek
A memorable novel about a lady and a pirate – their unique romance, their exciting adventures, their strange destiny

Kestle Barton
A beautiful old farm surrounded by orchards. The Meneage is famous for its apples. The path passes right in front of Kestle Barton Gallery which has art shows throughout the year.

Helford Village

Lower
Calamansack

Calamansack
House

Boathouse
Beach

Pedn
Billy

Bar Beach

Helford
Passage

The Pool

Helford River

Pengwedhen
Wood

Penarvon
Cove

Helford Pt

Padgagarrack
Wood

Treath

Kennels

Walk
6

Frenchman's Creek

West
Quay

Site of Iron
Age Round

Orchard Lane

Site of Iron
Age Round

Treveador
Farm

Helford
Village

Withian
Quay

Kestle

Under
Wood

Bosahan
Home
Farm

Lodge

Halvose

Slate
Breccia

Frenchman's
Pill

Manaccan

Walk 4
Frenchman's Creek
- 4km (2½ miles)
- 1–2 hours

Meneage
Methodist
Church

Highlane

Tregonwell
Mill

Lannarth
Gate Farm

Tregonwell

| 0 | 0.25km | 0.5km | 0.75km | 1km |
| ¼ mile | | ½ mile | | |

Walk 5

Helford Passage, Trebah, Carwinion & Glendurgan

Three gardens

HELFORD FERRY

❶ An 'on-demand' pedestrian ferry service runs between Helford Point & Helford Passage from Easter to the end of October. Bikes OK.
☎ (01326) 250770

BUS

No bus service to Helford Village but you can catch the Helston - Falmouth bus which will drop you in Mawnan Smith or at the entrance to the gardens (1 hour journey time from Helston). It's a steep walk down to Helford Passage from Trebah Cross.

FOOD & DRINKS

All the gardens have cafes. Pubs – Ferryboat Inn at Helford Passage & Red Lion in Mawnan Smith. Food shop in Mawnan Smith.

LOOK OUT FOR...

- Grebe Beach
- Trebah Garden
  ☎ (01326) 252200
- Glendurgan Garden
  ☎ (01326) 252020
- Carwinion Garden
  ☎ (01326) 250258
- Boat hire Helford Pass.
  ☎ (01326) 250770

We've borrowed this small section from our *Falmouth & Roseland Guidebook* because it's so easy to get to from the Lizard side on the Helford Ferry. **Helford Passage** is the main hub of the river in the summer. Just sitting on the small beach in front of the popular pub is enjoyable but if you're feeling the call of the sea you can hire a motor boat to explore the little creeks and quays further up the estuary. Children might groan at the thought of visiting gardens but there's actually lots to keep them happy. At **Trebah** paths meander down a sub-tropical valley garden past waterfalls and water gardens and under the enormous leaves of *Gunnera* plants. Visitors to Trebah can also use the private beach at **Polgwidden Cove** for picnics and swimming. At **Carwinion** you can wander through sensory gardens and around the bamboo collection before taking tea on the terrace. **Glendurgan** was created in the early years of the C19th by the Fox family, Quaker merchants and shipping agents. Returning sea captains would bring back seeds for the garden from their travels. There's a laurel maze and an adventure play area. At the bottom of the valley is the pretty little hamlet of **Durgan**, built as a utopian village with a tiny school

for local children. If gardens aren't your thing, then **Grebe** is one of the loveliest small beaches in Cornwall. Or simply walk up through the woods of Carwinion Valley to **Mawnan Smith**, and around to Anna Maria Creek.

0	0.25km	0.5km	0.75km
0	¼ mile		½ mile

FERRY · BOAT HIRE · ICE CREAMS

Helford Passage

Walk 5
Helford Gardens
- 6.5km (4 miles)
- 2–3 hours

Mawnan Smith

School

Lower Penpoll

Higher Penpoll

Durgan Cross

Carwinion Garden

Penpoll Mill

Trenarth Bridge

Bosveal

Anna Maria Creek

35 400

Carwinion Valley

Trebah Cross

Glendurgan

Bosloe

Budock Vean Hotel

Trebah Wartha

Trebah

Petrant Cove

Golf Course

Chycoose

Durgan

Grebe Beach

Bar Road

Robin's Cove

Porth Sawsen or Cow Beach

Porthallack Beach

Bar Beach

Polgwidden Cove (Trebah Beach)
Access from Trebah Gardens

Helford River

The Pool

Helford Passage

Padgagarrack Wood

Padgagarrack Cove

sahan Cove

Penarvon

Helford Pt

Walk 6

Around Helford & The Meneage

Helford Village, Manaccan & St Anthony-in-Meneage

Between river & sea

Helford

Manaccan

Lizard Point

GILLAN CREEK FERRY
'On-demand' from the pontoon at St Anthony. Runs 1 April to end Oct.
☎(01326) 231357

BUS
There's no bus service on this side of the Helford.

CAR PARKS
Large car park & loos at Helford Village. Parking in Manaccan is limited to the roadside & can be scarce. St Anthony has a small pay car park behind the church.

FOOD & DRINKS
Shipwright's Arms in Helford, New Inn & South Cafe in Manaccan. Food & snacks at Helford Post Office & Manaccan Stores. Cafes in Helford.

LOOK OUT FOR...
- See the fig tree growing out of the walls of Manaccan Church
- Gillan Creek Ferry & boat hire – Sailaway ☎(01326) 231357
- Bosahan Gardens ☎(01326) 231351

Places where estuaries meet the sea are always full of interest and surprise as they alternate between sheltered creek and cliff. This small area contains three of the most attractive villages in the Meneage – **Helford**, **Manaccan** and **St Anthony** – as well as a trio of little sandy beaches on the banks of the Helford.

Helford Village & Treath

Helford is the largest and prettiest village on the river – a haunt of the rich, the famous and the retired. It's busy in the summer but paths radiate in all directions and the crowds soon melt away. Every inch of the creek is lined with quays and it was once an important harbour. Treath was the original ferry landing place – '*treth*' is Cornish for *ferry* or *landing*. On Good Friday each year people descend to the shores of the river to go *trigging*, in other words collecting cockles and other shellfish. In Cornish *trig* is *ebb tide* and shellfish are sometimes called trig-meat. The river, with its secretive creeks and sparse population, was perfect for smuggling, landing brandy in the isolated coves or by slipping in among the busy trade on the river. The isolated customs house at Kennels was ransacked

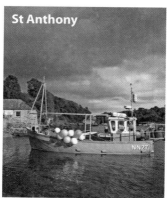

St Anthony

by smugglers in 1840. The excise men had confiscated contraband brandy in Coverack and it was 'reclaimed' by force, but the smugglers did leave a barrel for the customs men as rent.

The quays at Helford Village

The Dinas or Dennis Head

A natural place to set up a defence as it commands the entrance to the river (*dinas* is Cornish for *fort*). The first defences are thought to be Iron Age, about 2,500 years ago. This was a great period of fortifying cliffs and promontories and you'll come across cliff castles at Chynhalls and Lankidden south of Coverack. It's probable sites like these would only be occupied in times of trouble. The main prehistoric trade and power centre of the Helford was at Gear Camp and, like many similar important sites, it is discreetly tucked away at the head of a creek well out of sight of any raiders that might sail up the river. As different threats have materialised over the centuries so Dennis Head has been refortified. If it wasn't the Spanish it was the French, and if it wasn't either of them it was the English. During the English Civil War the headland was held for the King to protect the vital revenue from the tin trade.

Below
Little Egrets, once an unusual visitor, are now a common sight on the Helford. Less shy than their cousins the Grey Herons, they can often be seen using their quivering, out-sized feet to dislodge prey from the creek bed.

Above
A fig tree grows from the tower of Manaccan Church.
Below
Looking across The Bar towards St Anthony-in-Meneage. In theory, you can cross the creek here using the stepping stones that are uncovered for about an hour each side of low water. In practice, expect to wade across down stream or, for those who like to travel in style, you can call the ferry that runs from St Anthony in the summer months.

Bosahan Gardens & Cove

A lovely valley garden running down to Bosahan Cove, never crowded. Lots of southern hemisphere plants – azaleas and magnolias are out at Easter and you can wander through palm groves to Bosahan Cove on the river.

St Anthony-in-Meneage

Perhaps only St Just-in-Roseland can match the setting of this riverside hamlet and church. An 'on-demand' ferry runs from the pontoon to the other side of Gillan Creek during the summer for those following the coast path to Nare Point and Porthallow. You can also hire a motor boat, learn to sail dinghies or paddle a kayak up the river. If just the thought of that is too tiring you might simply want to sit on the pontoon with an ice cream. It's an early *lann* church (Cornish: *lann*, an *enclosed cemetery*) probably founded by the Celtic holy men and women of the C5th & C6th who travelled from Ireland and Wales. The farm next to the church is *Lantinning*, so it's possibly the *lann* or monastery of *Intenyn* which changed over the years to the more conventional *Anthony*. There's a small holy well at the back of the churchyard.

Manaccan

This is another early lann church and has a fig tree growing from the wall of the tower. It's been growing there for more than a hundred years and a superstition has grown up around it insisting it shouldn't be harmed or bad luck will come to the village. There is a fine thatched pub, the New Inn, with a beer garden that's perfect for children as well as the popular South Cafe.

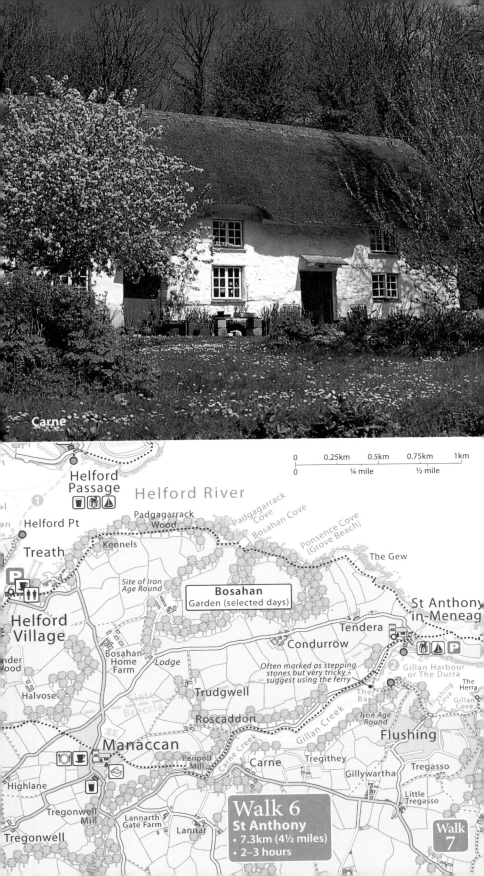

Carne

Helford
Passage

Helford River

Padgagarrack
Wood

Padgagarrack Cove

Bosahan Cove

Ponsence Cove
(Grove Beach)

Helford Pt

Treath

Kennels

The Gew

Site of Iron
Age Round

Bosahan
Garden (selected days)

St Anthony
in-Meneag

Helford
Village

Bosahan
Home
Farm

Lodge

Tendera

Condurrow

Gillan Harbour
or The Durra

The Herra

Often marked as stepping
stones but very tricky –
suggest using the ferry

The Bar

Gillian
Cove

Halvose

Flushing
Cove

Ander
Wood

Slate
Breccia

Trudgwell

Iron Age
Round

Roscaddon

Gillan Creek

Flushing

Manaccan

Carne Creek

Penpoll
Mill

Carne

Tregithey

Gillywartha

Tregasso

Highlane

Tregonwell
Mill

Lannarth
Gate Farm

Lannar

Little
Tregasso

Tregonwell

0   0.25km   0.5km   0.75km   1km
0   ¼ mile   ½ mile

Walk 6
St Anthony
• 7.3km (4½ miles)
• 2–3 hours

Walk
7

Walk 7

Porthallow to Gillan, Flushing & Nare Point

A dish of many ingredients

GILLAN CREEK FERRY
② 'On-demand' – open the sign at steps. Runs 1 April to end October.
☎(01326) 231357

BUS
Helston - St Keverne bus – nearest stop is at St Keverne 2.3km (1½ miles) south of Porthallow.

CAR PARKING
There's no parking at Gillan or Flushing, but Porthallow has a large car park on the beach.

FOOD & DRINKS
Pubs – Five Pilchards in Porthallow, New Inn in nearby Manaccan plus pubs & food shops in St Keverne. No shops or cafes in Gillan or Flushing.

LOOK OUT FOR...
• Look out the World War 2 bunker & pill boxes at Nare Point
• Picnic & peaceful swim at Men-aver Beach or Parbean Cove
• Gillan Creek Ferry & boat hire – Sailaway
  ☎(01326) 231357

Onto the open cliff for the first time in this book. North of Porthallow the views open up to Pendennis Castle, St Anthony Lighthouse, Nare Head (Veryan) and in the far distance, the humped shape of the Dodman. Nare Head and the Dodman are both made up of the same Roseland Breccia you are standing on – rafts of pillow lava and quartzite – and are part of the same earth movements that brought the Lizard to the surface.

Gillan or Carne Creek
Except for the beach car park at **Porthallow**, there's no parking anywhere in this area, so despite its obvious beauty it's slightly overlooked but once visited, **Gillan Creek** would feature on almost any list of top Cornish beauty spots. It's is a very beautiful little creek reminiscent of Percuil and some of the creeks on the Roseland. It's very similar in scale to Loe Pool which probably resembled Gillan Creek before the sand bar (Loe Bar) blocked the entrance.

Flushing & Gillan
Flushing is one of my favourite little coves – part open to the sea but also still part of the sheltered estuary. The concrete wall at the top of the beach is a World War 2 anti-invasion defence, although, to be honest,

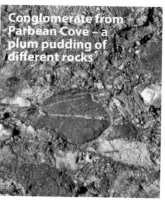

Conglomerate from Parbean Cove – a plum pudding of different rocks

it's hard to imagine it winning a fight with a Tiger tank. Gillan is one of those fortunate places, like Gunwalloe on the west coast, where the landscape is impressive in its arrangement but at the same time is

Looking across Gillan Harbour to Dennis Head

very human in scale. It has something to do with the combination of so many features in a small area: the distinctive shape of Dinas Head, its caves, the beaches at Flushing and Gillan and the little rocky headland of the Herra that juts out into the creek. The Bronze Age people had an unerring eye for these places and set up their barrows and cairns in these beauty spots. The fact that Gillan and Flushing are popular retreats full of expensive houses today perhaps reinforces the point.

The Herra.

Two Bronze Age barrows are recorded sitting on this little headland, although they're very difficult to make out. At least part of one has fallen into the sea as the cliff has eroded away. Cannon were sited here in the Civil War and again in World War 2.

Geology

You won't come onto the Lizard rocks properly until Porthallow but south of Gillan Creek at **Parbean Cove** & **Men-aver beach**, you start to see the impact of the Lizard as it was thrust north, up & over the slates of the Helford. The front edge of the Gondwanian continent acted like a bulldozer blade propelling a mile-wide slurry of jumbled rocks & pebbles. It's called a breccia or *olistostrome* – meaning *dish of many ingredients*. A curious plum pudding mix of rocks of very different age, composition & appearance (*photo left*).

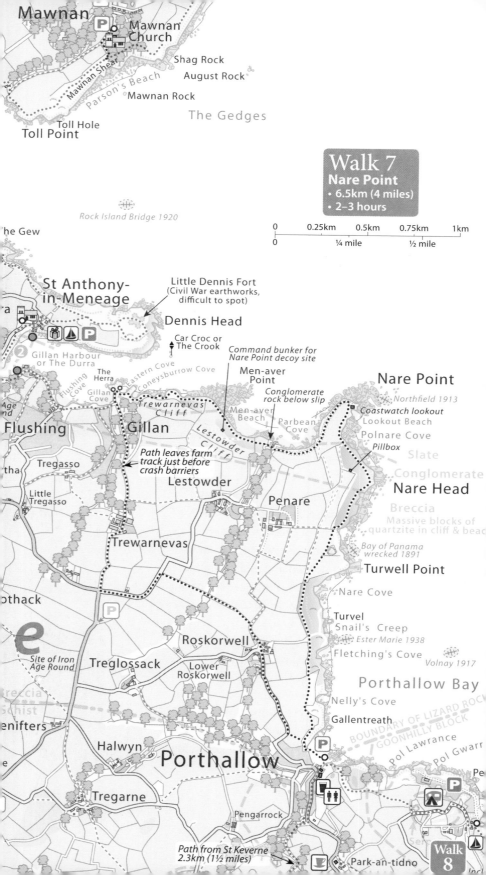

Nare Point & the site decoy

Ealing Film Studios built a set here in 1941 to draw attacking aircraft away from the important docks in Falmouth. It was controlled from a bunker on Lestowder Cliff (you can't get in but the entry hatch is still visible). Control wires and pulleys opened fake doors and windows simulating a poorly kept blackout. If an attack came in, flaming tar barrels gave the impression of buildings on fire.

The Bay of Panama is wrecked

The winter of 1890/91 was one of the worst in anyone's memory. Over Christmas there were seven weeks of frosts without a break. When the thaw suddenly arrived in March, the ice melted away almost overnight to be followed by a fortnight of balmy spring days. So when the Great Storm of 9–13 March blew in everyone was caught by surprise. Hurricane-force winds killed thousands of animals where they stood in the fields, freezing them in standing positions. Three ships foundered on the Manacles in a single day. The *Bay of Panama* with a crew of 40 and a cargo of jute from Calcutta, was running for the shelter of Falmouth Bay. They were almost safe when they were suddenly overwhelmed. Colossal waves rolled over the ship from stern to bow washing away the bridge and with it, the Captain, his wife and six crew. The surviving crew took to the rigging where many became frozen solid so the ropes had to be cut away to release their bodies. The next morning the wreck was discovered by a local farmer and the 17 surviving crew were rescued and put up for the night in St Keverne. They set off for Falmouth the next day on foot and without shoes, and had to be rescued for a second time after becoming trapped in snowdrifts.

Above
The lookout at Nare Point was for observing torpedo trials off the coast in tandem with the lookout at Porthkerris Cove. It's now used as a Coastwatch Station.
Below
The *Bay of Panama* is wrecked at Turwell Point. The weather was so cold that some of the crew froze solid to the rigging, which had to be cut away to recover their bodies.

Walk 8

Porthallow, Porthkerris, Porthoustock & St Keverne

Twin valleys & old stone quarries

Helston
Nare Head
Porthallow
St Keverne
Lizard Point

BUS

Helston - St Keverne bus. St Keverne stop.

CAR PARKS

Large car parks on the beaches at Porthallow & Porthoustock. St Keverne has some parking in the village square & on the road down to Tregonning. There is a pay car park at Porthkerris.

FOOD & DRINKS

Pubs – Three Tuns & White Hart in St Keverne, Five Pilchards in Porthallow. Fat Apple Cafe at Park-an-Tidno. Food shops in St Keverne, a small mobile cafe at Porthkerris in the summer (you do have to pay to park). Roskilly's on the south side of St Keverne for ice creams, teas & meals.

LOOK OUT FOR...

• Learn to dive at Porthkerris

Since quarrying started here in the 1890s, nearly every part of the cliffs between **Porthallow** and **Porthoustock** has been blasted away creating an eerie semi-industrial landscape. Activity peaked in the 1920s supplying stone for Cornwall's roads and there was a late flourish of activity in the early 1940s as airfields like Predannack were constructed across Cornwall. The West of England Quarry at Porthoustock is the only quarry still working. It supplies gabbro and basalt. Surprisingly large ships have to make their way gingerly around the top of the Manacles to load at the quay. It must be a bit like tip toeing through a graveyard at night.

Porthallow & Porthoustock

While neither are great beauty spots both are popular places with a very particular character. Early photos show Porthoustock and Porthallow as narrow inlets with boats drawn up on slips near the present-day roads. One hundred years of quarry spill has now left the sea 200 metres away. Officially, the coast path turns inland between Porthoustock and Porthallow, a legacy of when the quarries were active, but as they have been abandoned for

Trenoweth Woods

decades, there is a well used but unofficial path, making its way past abandoned silos, tramways and inclines. A few small boats work the reefs and ledges from both villages. The boats are hauled

Porthallow

up onto the beach by winch. An old fish cellar or 'pilchard palace' where the pilchards were stacked and pressed before being packed into barrels for export to southern Europe, sits by the side of the Five Pilchards Inn at Porthallow. The beach sheds at Porthoustock are said to have been constructed from corrugated iron sheets salvaged from the *Glenbervie*, wrecked on Lowland Point in 1902. Both coves link to **St Keverne** by old paths that follow wooded valleys inland.

Porthkerris

This is the main base for divers on the Lizard. Novices can scuba dive from the beach on the inshore reefs. More experienced divers roam the wrecks in the deep water around the Manacles. The large observation building was used to monitor torpedo trials in Falmouth Bay in tandem with the lookout on Nare Head.

Geology

The boundary of the Lizard rocks is on the south side of **Porthallow beach** where you can see large boulders of Old Lizard Head Schist that have fallen from the cliff. Slices of this rock pop all along the main boundary of the Lizard. Also on the beach are blocks of serpentine with their characteristic fissured rind. They're part of block of deformed cumulate rocks, formed near the Moho, that outcrop between **Porthallow** & **Porthkerris**. South of Porthkerris to **Porthoustock** you can see the blue and white layered rocks of the Traboe Schists – deformed gabbro.

ewarnevas Cliff

Men-aver Beach

rock below slip

Parbean Cove

Northfield 1913

Coastwatch lookout
Lookout Beach
Polnare Cove

Pillbox

Lestowder Cliff

Slate

Conglomerate

Nare Head

Lestowder

Penare

Breccia
Massive blocks of quartzite in cliff & beach

rnevas

Walk 7

Bay of Panama wrecked 1891

Turwell Point

Nare Cove

Walk 8
Quarry Walk
- 6.5km (4 miles)
- 2–3 hours

0	0.25km	0.5km	0.75km	1k
0	¼ mile		½ mile

Roskorwell

Turvel
Snail's Creep

Ester Marie 1938

Fletching's Cove

Volnay 1917

Lower Roskorwell

ck

Porthallow Bay

Nelly's Cove

Path leaves beach by red buoy

Gallentreath

BOUNDARY OF LIZARD ROCKS
GOONHILLY BLOCK

Pol Lawrance

Pol Gwarra

Traboe Cumulates
(recrystallised rocks from near the Moho)

Porthallow

Pedn Tiere

Porthkerris Point

Drawna Rocks

Pengarrock

Old MOD lookout

Porthkerris Cove

Serpentine

Clara 1859

Old tramway

Park-an-tidno

Incline

*Nuestra Senora de B
St Quintera 1807*

regarne Mill

Tregaminion

Official Coast Path

Trenance

St Keverne Quarries
(schist, disused)

Incline

Men Talhac

Pencra Hea

Levellers

Tr

Tredinnick

Schist

The Holts

Chyreen

Arrow

Georgina 18

Sweet May 19

Trenoweth Farm

Quartzite

Trenoweth Mill

Batty's Point

e

Porthoustoc

*Path leaves
St Keverne via churchyard*

Trenoweth Valley

Treloyan

West of England Quarry
(gabbro, in use)

Ve
R

The G

Man
M

Well Lane

Parc-an-grouse

Giant's Quoits

Dulgee
Rocks

e

Rosenithon
(No parking)

Little Treginges

Orchard

Leggan Cove

Gabbro fract
by numero
black dyk

School Hill

Long Meadow Nature Trail

Walk 9

Leggan Point

Godrevy Cove

*HMS Primrose 1809
the loss of 120 onl
survivor - a drumn
boy. Lost on the sa
night as the Dispa
on Lowland Point*

Trelyn

Trythance

Shag Rock

Tregellast Barton

Dean Quarry
(gabbro, disused)

Dean Point

Cabin

Roskilly's

Treglohan

St Keverne & The Manacles

St Keverne started life as a Celtic monastery 1,000 years ago probably at a site at nearby Tregonning. A few stone fragments are inside St Keverne church. It's the largest settlement in the Meneage and is surrounded by some of the most productive (gabbro) soils in Cornwall. The mild Lizard climate allows farmers to get their crops to market a few weeks ahead of the rest of the country. In the winter, the fields around Trenoweth are full of early daffodils ready to give a little Cornish cheer to city office workers. You can't see the sea from St Keverne but you can smell it, it's never far away. The churchyard has many memorials to victims of wrecks on the Manacles. They've claimed almost as many victims as Lizard Point.

The Mohegan is lost

She struck Vase Rock at full speed on the evening of 14 October 1898 just as her passengers were sitting down to dinner. A gash tore down one side flooding the generators, immediately throwing the ship into darkness and panic. Her momentum carried her forward to the Maen Varses where she sank just a few minutes later with many passengers trapped in the dining room. 106 were drowned out of a total of 157 passengers and crew.

Above
The spire of St Keverne Church pops unexpectedly into view from the surrounding countryside. It acts as a navigation marker for ships passing the Manacles (Cornish: *maen* is *rocks* and *eglos* is *church*).
Below
Victims of the wreck of the *Mohegan* are interred in St Keverne churchyard.

HILLY SHEET
A SHEET
Dalhousie 1884
n Chynoweth or The Morah
r Cross 1787
Ringdove 1829
Gabbro
Maen Garrick
Sarah Jane 1823
Gwinges
Princess Charlotte 1802
Vase Rock
nacles   *Rose 1838*
Penwin Reef   Manacles bell buoy
strel
ock
Spyridion Vagliano 1890
Mohegan wrecked 1898 with the loss of 106
Maen Varses or The Voices
Carn-du Rocks
no 1915

Walks
9 & 10

Coverack, Lowland Point, Roskilly's & The Manacles
Ice creams, prehistoric pots & sacred crag

Helston
Porthallow
St Keverne
Coverack

Lizard Point

BUS
Helston - Coverack -
St Keverne bus. Coverack
bus shelter or St Keverne
stops.

CAR PARKING
Car park (& loos) at North
Corner & small car park
at Dolor Point (both
Coverack). There's also
parking for visitors to
Roskilly's & some roadside
parking at Treglohan plus
a few spaces at Giant's
Quoit & near Dean Quarry.

FOOD & DRINK
Roskilly's for ice creams,
teas & meals. Coverack
has the Bay Hotel &
Paris Hotel (seaside beer
garden) & cafes. Food
shop at the General Stores
in Coverack & in
St Keverne.

LOOK OUT FOR...
- Watch milking & ice
  cream making at
  Roskilly's plus Long
  Meadow Nature Trail
- Picnic & wild flowers at
  Lowland Point
- Pebbles in Coverack
  Cove
- Coverack Windsurf
  Centre

Coverack is a place of many pleasures. It's a mecca
for geologists who come to study the rocks on **Mill
Beach** – pebble heaven – and for botanists who come
to study the plants on the way to **Lowland Point** – a
flower heaven. You might enjoy a windsurf in the
bay, a stroll around the harbour with an ice cream,
to browse the craft shops or sit with a drink in the
seaside beer garden of the Paris Hotel.

Coverack
This is the last naturally sheltered harbour until St
Michael's Mount. The pier has a charming enclosing
arm very much like the Old Pier at Newlyn. In the
C19th this was a big pilchard fishery as the handsome
pilchard cellars behind the Paris Hotel show. The
pilchard shoals have long since left but a fleet of
small boats work from here sharing the harbour with
windsurfers, canoeists and dinghy sailors. A lifeboat
was stationed in Coverack until 1963 because of the
danger of the **Manacles**. At high water the reef is all
but invisible but as the tide drops you can almost hear
a snarl as the rocks emerge like bared teeth.

Roskilly's
Tregellast Barton, just south of St Keverne village,

is the home of
wonderful Roskilly's
Ice Cream. There
are craft shops, a
restaurant and you
can watch the ice
cream being made. A
trail follows the stream
down the valley past
wildlife pools to
Godrevy Cove.

Coverack Harbour with Lowland Point in the background

Lowland Point & Carrick Crane Crags

The walk from North Corner to Lowland Point in the late spring and summer is a Lizard highlight. It's famous for the range and number of flowers. The crags above Lowland Point seem to have had a significance for the Stone Age inhabitants of this area. Neolithic pottery from about 4,000 years ago was discovered in a cave below Carrick Crane Rock in 1918. This type of pottery, called *Grooved Ware*, is associated with monuments like henges and with burial sites in southern England and therefore seems to have had some ritual importance. We know from other sites that caves were important places for ritual in the Stone Age and similar fragments of Grooved Ware have been found in the crevices at Logan Rock on the Land's End peninsula. The opening at Carrick Crane rock is visible (but a scramble) and it's worth a detour from the coast path. The sherds are in the Royal Cornwall Museum.

Below & left
The *SS Ocklinge* hard & fast on Lowland Point in March 1932. The Captain dumped part of the cargo of iron ore overboard in an attempt to float her off the reef. It's still there scattered between the boulders slowly rusting away. It didn't work & she became a total loss.

Trevallack Laddenvean Well Lane Parc-an-grouse Rosenit
(No parkir

St Keverne 🅿 ☕ 🚻 School Hill Little Treginges Orchard Coast path heads inland at Godrevy Cove

Porthousrock Stream Sch Long Meadow Nature Trail Trythance

Treskewe Trelyn 🅿 Tregellast Barton 🅿 Dean Quarry (gabbro, disused)

Walk 9
Roskilly's Stroll
- 3.1km (2 miles)
- 1–2 hours

Roskilly's ☕ 🍴 🎁 Treglohan

B3293 Chywoone Trevean Short cut to Roskilly's Polcr Bea

Main Dale Trebarveth *SS Go 1928* *Dis 180*

Trevalsoe Carrick Crane Rock Low

Boscarnon *T h e   G r o v e* Carrick Crane Crags *H.G Gre Ockli*

36 Gilly Tregod *(abandoned farm)* *Mina Cantaquin 1955* The Oar

B3294 Kilter Davas

Pedn-myin *Affleck 1838* Trebarveth Romano-British salt works. Easy to miss on the cliff edge the remains of ovens to evaporate salt water. The Cornish Sea Salt Company do a similar thing today at Porthkerris.

North Corner *Gabbro (Oceanic crust)*

🚻🅿 Coverack bus shelter *Transition Zone Mohorovičic discontinuity*

The Bay Coverack Cove

Mill Beach 🍴🍺⚓ *Serpentine (Upper Mantle)*

🅿 Dolor Point Paris Hotel *Archangelos 1929*

Walk 10
Lowland Point
- 8.2km (5 miles)
- 3–4 hours

erack 🚻 Perprean Cove The Oxen *Rose 1866* *Omer Denise 1932*

Chynhalls Farm Polgravel *Pindos 1912* Guthens

Headlands Chynhalls (Mear) Point

Walk 10 Mears Beach Porthbeer Cove

Chynhalls Cliff *Serpentine (Upper Mantle)*

Goldolphin 1888

| | 0 | 0.25km | 0.5km | 0.75km | 1km |
| 0 | | ¼ mile | | ½ mile | |

Luz
Manacle Pt
Mildran's
Rock
Dulgevean
Rocks

Gabbro

Maen Garrick
Sarah Jane 1823

Gwinges
Princess Charlotte 1802

Vase Rock

Rose 1838

Manacles
bell buoy

bro fractured
y numerous
black dykes

imrose1809 with
of 120 only one
r - a drummer
st on the same
s the Dispatch
land Point

Manacles

Minstrel
Rock

Penwin Reef

Spyridion Vagliano 1890

Mohegan wrecked 1898
with the loss of 106

Cabinet 1872

Maen Varses or The Voices

Carn-du Rocks

SS Juno 1915

Mormon Maid 1851

recked 1855 with the
120 lives (buried in
rne Churchyard)

John & Rebecca 1867

nsport ship Dispatch, with a detachment
th Hussars, returning home from the
ular War wrecked on Lowland Point with
of 104, only 7 survived.

a

The Paris is grounded

The *City of Paris* was one of the swiftest steam ships ever built – a three times winner of the Blue Riband for the fastest Atlantic crossing. In May 1899 she ran aground on Lowland Point having lost her way in fog. Miraculously, she must have steamed straight through the Manacles past the *Mohegan* – wrecked only a few months before with the loss of 106. Many victims were still entombed inside the ship with only the tolling of the Manacles bell buoy for company (it still tolls today). Thankfully for the *Paris* there was only a slight sea running and all her passengers and crew were saved, in dreadful contrast to the heavy loss of life on the *Mohegan*. The *Paris* was pulled free and towed to Belfast for repair, resuming service as the *SS Philadelphia*.

The Paris grounded on Lowland Point, in the foreground the masts of the Mohegan.

Geology

You may notice some odd behaviour on Mill Beach – people apparently staring at their feet, moving on suddenly then stopping to stare at their feet again. They're studying the transition zone between the rocks of the Earth's deep interior (serpentine) and the rocks of the thin outer crust above (gabbro & basalt). These unusual rocks are normally found 7–10km down so it's very rare to find them at the surface. This whole area is a vertical slice of oceanic crust tipped on its side by earth movements. As you walk north towards Lowland Point & the Manacles, you're walking towards the surface. Turn south from Coverack, towards Chynhalls Point & Black Head then, like Orpheus, you're descending into the underworld. The rocks that come from here, like serpentine, form a strange & sombre landscape which you will experience as you move further south.

Looking over Pentreath Beach to Old Lizard Head & the Man O'War reef. To the right of the figures on the beach you can see the boiler of the *SS Maud* wrecked here in 1912.

2. Lizard Point & the far south
Coverack, Cadgwith, Lizard Point & Kynance

THIS IS THE LIZARD at its most undiluted and unrestrained – a very impressive landscape quite unlike anything else in Cornwall. It's a parade of beautiful coves and beaches – **Downas**, **Carleon**, **Housel**, **Pentreath** and **Kynance** – as well as a roll call of fearsome cliffs like **The Rill** and **Vellan Head**. The first real taste of serpentine scenery comes south of Coverack on the cliffs at **Black Head** and **Downas Cove**. Between **Kennack Sands** and **Landewednack** the cliffs are interspersed with small coves and shallow wooded valleys like **Gwendreath** and **Poltesco** that then stretch up onto **Goonhilly Downs**. It's a coastline of tiny isolated beaches and coves once popular with smugglers and brigands.

Lizard Point takes the full brunt of gales that spin and spiral north from the Equator. Floundering sailing ships were once driven onto the reefs and into the high cliffs. Hundreds of wrecks and thousands of bodies have been washed ashore on this coast. Any cliff that has soil deep enough to hold a shallow grave has been pressed into service.

On the west coast around **Kynance** and **Pentreath**, heathland reaches down to cloak the cliff slopes. In the summer the grassy cliffs are full of the colours of nodding *Harebells*, varieties of clover on the schist soils and a seaside riot of daisies and *Bird's-foot Trefoil*. It's a multicoloured rebuke to the sombre and brooding serpentine cliffs. At **Mullion Cliff** the serpentine reaches a thundering crescendo and at **Polurrian**, we finally leave the Lizard rocks behind crossing onto the slates that create a more familiar Cornish seaside scenery.

GETTING AROUND
BUS
This section is served by two bus routes from Helston. The Helston - Lizard Town bus (**37**) via Mullion & the main beaches. The Helston - St Keverne & Coverack bus (**36**) also goes past Goonhilly Earth Station & Traboe Cross.

Serpentine workshop at Lizard Point

HIGHLIGHTS...
- Heath in bloom in July & August on Lizard & Predannack Downs
- Boat trips from Mullion Cove, Coverack & Cadgwith

PLACES TO VISIT
- Lizard Lighthouse Heritage Centre
- Lizard Wireless Station

PLACES TO EAT
- Coverack has a pub, cafes & restaurants
- Cadgwith has a cafe & food at the pub with singing on Fridays & beach barbecues in the summer

Walks 11&12

Coverack, Black Head & Downas Cove
Black cliffs of the east coast

BUS
Helston - Coverack - St Keverne bus. Coverack bus shelter stop at North Corner. Instead of returning to Coverack on a circular walk you can pick up the bus again at Kuggar above Kennack Sands on the Helston - Lizard Town service. That would make an 8.5km one way walk from Coverack bus shelter at North Corner.

CAR PARKS
Large car park at North Corner, small car park at Dolor Point (both Coverack). Small National Trust parking area at Treleaver (4 or 5 cars only).

FOOD & DRINKS
Paris Hotel (seaside beer garden) & cafes in Coverack. Food shop at the General Stores in Coverack.

LOOK OUT FOR...
- Shoot the breeze at Downas Cove
- Swim at Mears Beach
- Picnic on Chynhalls Point or Downas Cove
- Boat trip from the harbour at Coverack

As you walk south from Coverack towards **Chynhalls** you can be in no doubt you have left the Meneage. Gone are the intimate wooded creeks and rich farmland. For the first time you encounter the scenery of serpentine. Crags glower down at you as you walk past **Perprean** and **Polgravel**. This is an altogether less soft and contented landscape. The cliffs build towards **Black Head** and **Pedn Boar** then ease down towards the beach at **Downas Cove**. It's a taste of what's in store on the more exposed serpentine cliffs of the west coast – the magnificent black cliffs of Vellan Head and The Rill.

Chynhalls Point & cliff castle
This is one of two cliff castles on this stretch of coast, the other is at nearby Lankidden. The earth ramparts are clearly visible. We know from excavations at other sites that the ramparts often had timber palisades on top of the bank. They date from the later part of the Iron Age, which seems to have been a time of increased piracy and raiding. They may have been pressed back into use when the Saxons and Vikings invaded eastern and northern England pushing many Britons before them – a cause of the great Celtic migrations to Brittany in the C5th and C6th.

Downas Cove
The valley behind is beautiful on a summer day and it's a good place to stop and do a bit of prospecting on the strand line. Sand is exposed for an hour or two each side of low water when there's a chance to paddle in the sandy pools and examine the serpentine where the sand and sea have polished the rock. The south-facing cliffs teem with butterflies.

0	0.25km	0.5km	0.75km	1km
0		¼ mile	½ mile	

Downas Cove

Penhallick Farm

Coverack

Dolor Point

Paris Hotel

Archangelos 1929

Trevothen

Penmarth Farm *Sch*

YHA

Little Trevothen

Perprean Cove

The Oxen

Rose 1866

Omer Denise 1932

Cold War nuclear bunker

Chynhalls Farm

Polgravel

Pindos 1912

Pendnavounder

Headlands

Guthens

Trewillis

Chynhalls (Mear) Point

Mears Beach

Porthbeer Cove

Walk 12
Black Head
• 6.3km (4 miles)
• 3–4 hours

Treleaver Cottage

Chynhalls Cliff

Walk 11
Chynhalls Stroll
• 2.6km (1½ miles)
• 1–2 hours

Treleaver

Tremorna

Old copper mine workings in cliff

Goldolphin 1888

Ebber Rocks

Plantagenet 1897

Briel 1792

Meludjack
Eagles Cove

Old lookout

Black Head

reathe

gles
nt

The Bees

Beagles Hole

Treleaver Cliff

Dinas Cove

Hyrlas Rock

Gunvor 1912

Dispatch 1809

Clan Alpine 1873

Pedn Boar

Kennack Sands & Lankidden Cove

Childhood memories & cliff castles

Helston

Coverack

Lankidden
Kennack Sands

Lizard Point

BUS
Helston - Lizard Town bus. Kuggar stop is about 15mins walk from Kennack Sands. You can also pick up the Helston - St Keverne bus at Coverack (8.5km) or by walking north over Goonhilly Downs to pick it up at Traboe Cross or the Earth Station stop (about a 6km walk).

CAR PARKS
There's a large car park at Kennack Sands – always busy on sunny days in the school holidays.

FOOD & DRINKS
Kennack Sands has a couple of beach shops.

LOOK OUT FOR...
• Poldowrian Garden & museum (open on occasional days in spring & summer)
• Pond dipping behind Kennack Sands
• Shingle plants at the top of the beach
• Picnic at Lankidden Cliff Castle & a swim at Lankidden Cove
• Inland walks onto Goonhilly Downs

As well as the beach, which is the most popular on this side of the Lizard, there's plenty to explore at Kennack Sands with cliff walks in either direction and the chance to walk inland onto **Goonhilly Downs**. We've highlighted a short walk to **Lankidden Cove** where you can picnic inside the cliff castle or, if the tide is out, at the cove below. Compass Cove and Spernic Cove aren't readily accessible from the cliff path.

Kennack Sands
This is a great beach for families and a good place for inexperienced body boarders and surfers because it's less exposed to big Atlantic swells than the west coast beaches like Poldhu. For beachcombers, there are plenty of interesting pebbles – serpentine and pink Kennack Gneiss are the most colourful. At the top of the beach there's a good selection of seaside plants like *Sea Rocket* and several varieties of *Orache*, one with beautiful frosted leaves. The reedy pool at the back of the beach (*Kennack* or *Keunek* is Cornish for *reed bed*) has boardwalks so the children can go pond dipping in the summer and it's often buzzing with dragonflies. Basking sharks, easily identified by their twin black fins and languid swimming style,

The falling tide at Poldowrian reveals a ship's boiler.

are often seen here in the summer. An adult will grow to 15 metres long and they frequently come very close to the cliffs, trawling the inshore waters for plankton released from barnacles and mussels.

Kennack Sands with the Caerverracks reef in the middle distance. Eastern Cliffs, Lankidden & Pedn Boar in the background.

Poldowrian

As you walk along the cliff towards Lankidden you'll come across a tiny valley sandwiched between serpentine crags with just enough shelter for a seaside garden – this is Poldowrian. There's no access from the cliff path and it only opens on occasional days for the Cornwall Gardens Trust or to raise money for Cornwall Wildlife Trust – check their websites for details. In 1965 a cliff fire revealed the stone walls of a 7,500 year old Mesolithic settlement. One of the farmyard barns has a display of finds – it's usually open on garden days. The falling tide reveals a ship's boiler on the beach below Poldowrian Valley. I'm not aware of a wreck on this site; it's possible that it's from the *Normand* wrecked on Caerverracks Reef in 1914. The thick-walled boilers often remain intact long after the rest of a wreck has been flattened (see *SS Maud* on Pentreath) and are sometimes rolled along the coast by storms.

The promontory at **Lankidden** is a finger of gabbro in the serpentine cliffs. It is possibly the remains of a great underground fissure in the serpentine that fed the gabbro to the north of Coverack. There are very beautiful examples of sheared & deformed gabbro in Lankidden Cove.

Flora

An interesting area because of the variety of habitats – shingle beach, dunes, exposed & grassy cliffs. Among the boulders at the top of the beach at Kennack Sands you'll find spear leaved & frosted *Orache & Sea Rocket*. Behind the anti-tank wall above Eastern Beach there's a prostrate form of *Bittersweet*, a member of the potato family. The grassy slopes of Lankidden are very colourful & on the way down to the cove you'll see some of the plants of exposed cliffs like *Rock Samphire & Thrift*.

Frosted Orache at Kennack Sands

Bittersweet above Eastern Beach

Lankidden Cove

This is one of those lovely little sandy coves that you occasionally chance upon when you're walking the cliffs. If you're lucky, the tide will be out as the beach is only uncovered for a few hours each side of low water. It's a bit of a scramble down.

Lankidden Cliff Castle

An obvious defensive site protected on the landward side by some impressive earth ramparts. It seems unlikely that it was a permanent settlement because it has no water supply and it's so exposed (just like Chynhalls). Some cliff castles are known to have been used as trading places but most are thought to have functioned as temporary refuges from Irish and Viking raiders. They usually date to around the last part of the Iron Age (2,700 years ago).

Trelan bronze mirror

This beautiful mirror was discovered in 1833 in a grave north of Trelan along with other brooches, beads and bracelets. It's Iron Age, so the person who owned it would have seen Lankidden Cliff Castle when it was active and may have acquired it there from traders. Burials from this time are rare, the usual practice being to expose the dead in the open. It's in the British Museum.

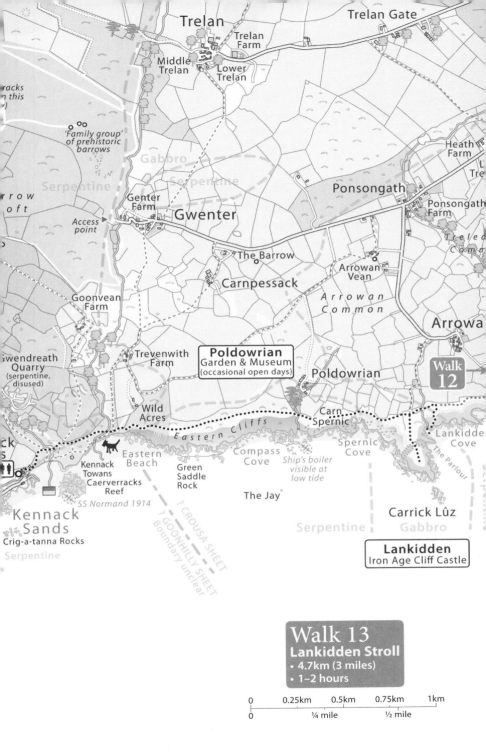

Trelan

Trelan Gate

Trelan Farm

Middle Trelan

Lower Trelan

'Family group' of prehistoric barrows

Heath Farm

Gabbro

Serpentine

Serpentine

Ponsongath

Ponsongath Farm

row oft

Genter Farm

Access point

Gwenter

The Barrow

Arrowan Vean

Treleo Comm

Carnpessack

Arrowan Common

Goonvean Farm

Arrowa

Trevenwith Farm

Poldowrian
Garden & Museum
(occasional open days)

Poldowrian

Walk 12

Gwendreath Quarry
(serpentine, disused)

Wild Acres

Eastern Cliffs

Carn Spernic

Lankidde Cove

The Parlour

ck s

Eastern Beach

Kennack Towans
Caerverracks Reef

Compass Cove

Spernic Cove

Green Saddle Rock

Ship's boiler visible at low tide

SS Normand 1914

Kennack Sands

Crig-a-tanna Rocks

Serpentine

The Jay

Carrick Lûz

Serpentine

Gabbro

? CROUSA SHEET

? GOONHILLY SHEET
Boundary unclear

Lankidden
Iron Age Cliff Castle

Walk 13
Lankidden Stroll
• 4.7km (3 miles)
• 1–2 hours

| 0 | 0.25km | 0.5km | 0.75km | 1km |

| 0 | ¼ mile | ½ mile |

Walks 14 & 15

Goonhilly Downs
Stargazing & solitude

Helston
Goonhilly
Erisey
Poltesco
Lizard Point

BUS
Helston - Mawgan - Coverack - St Keverne service. Goonhilly stop. Helston - Lizard Town service. Mullion Holiday Village stop on the west side of the downs, 3.9km (2½ miles) from Goonhilly.

CAR PARKING
National Nature Reserve car park at Goonhilly plus small lay-bys at Croft Pascoe & Bray's Cot for those who want to wander the Downs.

FOOD & DRINKS
Nothing in this immediate area but pub & food shops in St Keverne & Mullion plus the Wheel Inn at Cury Cross Lanes.

LOOK OUT FOR...
• Best in the late summer when the downs are dry & the heather & gorse are in flower
• Follow the stream from Goonhilly to Erisey & then down to Poltesco Cove
• Pools full of tadpoles in January at Croft Pascoe Forest

I suspect opinion has always been sharply divided over Goonhilly – you either like it or you don't. For some, it's a bleak and dreary waste fit only for witches, ghosts and highway robbers. For others, it's an exhilarating, strange and absorbing place. Whatever your view, it is without doubt the spiritual heart of the Lizard and one of the few places in Cornwall where you can taste silence and solitude.

Its strangeness comes partly from the contrast between the satellite dishes of the Earth Station and the heathland. But stranger still is the realisation that the Earth Station sits on the focal point of a huge prehistoric ritual landscape that extends in all directions and whose boundaries reach as far as Predannack Downs, Kynance Heights and Barrow Croft – all of which are great walks from here. An array of invisible threads tie groups of barrows back to **Dry Tree** menhir and **Cruc Drænoc** (Cornish: *cruc* is *barrow* and *dreynek* is *thorny*). Barrows (man-made earth mounds) are usually, but not always, associated with the burial of an individual.

The Lizard is, at one and the same time, remarkable for its prehistoric monuments and

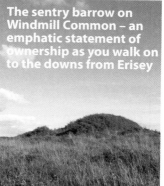

The sentry barrow on Windmill Common – an emphatic statement of ownership as you walk on to the downs from Erisey

oddly missing types found elsewhere in Cornwall. Where are the early prehistoric monuments, the circles, entrance graves and quoits that populate the neighbouring Land's End Peninsula? Perhaps the Lizard

Goonhilly Earth Station

was too thinly populated then or the hunter gatherer lifestyle continued here while pioneer farmers (and their monuments) got going on the moors of Penwith. Whatever the reason, by the time of the later Bronze Age, about 4,000 years ago, the downs were heavily populated with barrows. These people had a fascination with the stars and the seasons possibly because they were skilled mariners. I think the Bronze Age kings would have approved of the huge satellite dishes sending messages to deep space missions while they lay in their barrows staring up at the stars attempting to do the same.

The best way to arrive on the downs is on foot from the coast either by **Erisey** or from **Kennack Sands**. It's often difficult walking, invariably boggy even in summer. As you leave the last trees and stream behind you're presented with a tall 'sentry' barrow on Windmill Common, one of the tallest but least visited.

Flora

Most of the Downs are National Nature Reserves. Goonhilly is a classic for the Lizard flora. Around the area of the National Nature Reserve car park you'll find information boards & all the plants of the serpentine heaths – Saw-wort, Great Burnet (*below*), Cornish Heath.

Above
Dry Tree Menhir. A Bronze Age standing stone at the geographical & spiritual heart of the Lizard. It's a gabbro rock presumably chosen & hauled here from the boulders on Crousa Downs – about 3 miles away. Excavations elsewhere in Britain have uncovered Bronze Age ropes made from Honeysuckle stems.

Below
World War 2 anti-glider defences on Goonhilly Downs. The bases once held upright poles.

Cruc Drænoc & the Dry Tree menhir

Dry Tree is the highest point on the Downs and the central point not only in the prehistoric landscape – burial mounds surround and radiate from here – but the meeting point of five parishes and the site of public hangings, particularly of highwaymen. It is said, mostly in pubs late at night, that the ghosts of highwaymen hanged at Dry Tree still haunt the downs preying on any person foolish enough to venture across the downs at night. At night a ghostly white ship with billowing sails may be seen floating on Croft Pascoe Pool.

RAF Dry Tree

This was an early warning station for RAF Predannack during World War 2 and part of a long chain of radar installations along the south coast of Britain including a similar one at nearby Trelanvean. The brick buildings around the National Nature Reserve car park are associated with it and you can walk onto the roof of the receiver block where there are information boards and you can get wide views across the downs.

Goonhilly Earth Station

The Earth Satellite Station continues the long tradition of communications installations on the Lizard, pioneered by the maritime telegraph station at Bass Point and the transatlantic radio station at Poldhu. Built in the early 1960s, it was for many years the busiest and largest satellite station on Earth, relaying millions of telephone calls, television links and internet services every day. That role has ended and the site is now likely to be used for deep space communication with spacecraft and as a space research centre.

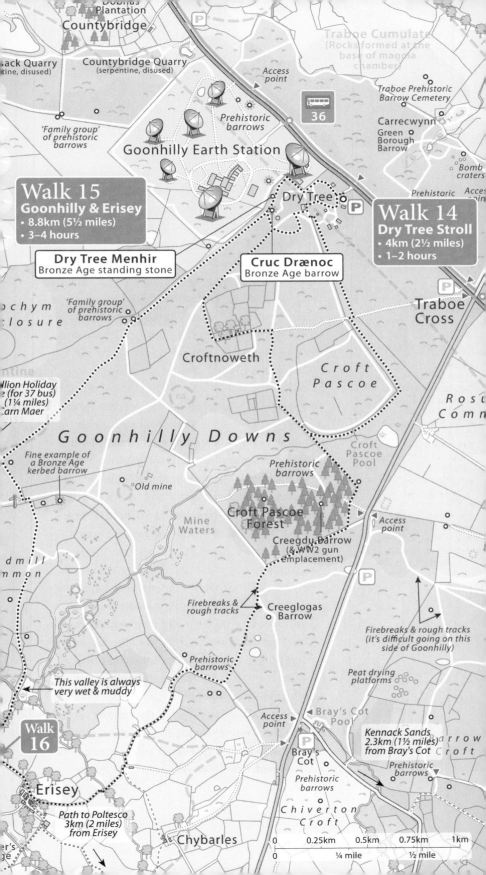

Countybridge
Dobhas Plantation

'ack Quarry
(ine, disused)

Countybridge Quarry
(serpentine, disused)

Traboe Cumulate
(Rocks formed at the base of magma chamber)

Access point

Prehistoric barrows

36

Traboe Prehistoric Barrow Cemetery

'Family group' of prehistoric barrows

Carrecwynn
Green Borough Barrow

Goonhilly Earth Station

Prehistoric barrows

Bomb craters

Prehistoric Acces

Dry Tree

P

Walk 15
Goonhilly & Erisey
• 8.8km (5½ miles)
• 3–4 hours

Dry Tree Menhir
Bronze Age standing stone

Cruc Drænoc
Bronze Age barrow

P

Walk 14
Dry Tree Stroll
• 4km (2½ miles)
• 1–2 hours

Traboe Cross

ochym losure

'Family group' of prehistoric barrows

Croftnoweth

Croft Pascoe

Ros Comn

ntine

llion Holiday
e (for 37 bus)
(1¼ miles)
arn Maer

G o o n h i l l y   D o w n s

Fine example of a Bronze Age kerbed barrow

Old mine

Prehistoric barrows

KG

Croft Pascoe Pool

Mine Waters

Croft Pascoe Forest

Creegdu Barrow
(& WW2 gun emplacement)

Access point

dmill mmon

Firebreaks & rough tracks

Creeglogas Barrow

P

Firebreaks & rough tracks (it's difficult going on this side of Goonhilly)

Prehistoric barrows

Peat drying platforms

This valley is always very wet & muddy

Bray's Cot Pool

Walk 16

Access point

P

Bray's Cot

Kennack Sands 2.3km (1½ miles) from Bray's Cot

rrow Croft

Prehistoric barrows

Erisey

Prehistoric barrows

Path to Poltesco 3km (2 miles) from Erisey

Chybarles

C h i v e r t o n   C r o f t

r's je

0	0.25km	0.5km	0.75km	1km
0	¼ mile		½ mile	

Walks 16 & 17

Poltesco, Carleon Cove, Cadgwith & Erisey

Fish & saints

Helston
Goonhilly
Erisey
Poltesco
Cadgwith
Lizard Point

BUS
Helston - Lizard Town bus. At the top of the walk, get off at Mullion Holiday Village & walk 1.8km (1¼ miles) down the country road to Erisey. At the bottom of the walk, get off at Ruan Minor or Kuggar stops. If you keep going on to the downs from Erisey you can pick up the Helston - St Keverne bus at Goonhilly or Traboe Cross.

CAR PARKS
National Trust car park at Poltesco, small lay-by at Polstangey Bridge. Large public car park above Cadgwith. Avoid driving down the hill from Ruan Minor through Cadgwith village - it's very narrow & steep with lots of bottlenecks.

FOOD & DRINKS
Cadgwith Cove Hotel (pub) & cafe in Cadgwith Beach barbecues in the summer.

LOOK OUT FOR...
- Pebbles at Poltesco
- Singing at the Cadgwith Cove Hotel
- Beach barbecues at Cadgwith

Like all the valleys on the east side of the Lizard, **Ruan Valley**, in which **Cadgwith** sits, and **Poltesco Valley** are hollowed out of the Kennack Gneiss. The soil is noticeably more fertile here than on the surrounding sea of serpentine. We've picked out a very enjoyable walk from **Carleon Cove** to **Erisey** where you are within touching distance of Goonhilly Downs. As you progress up the valley from Poltesco, the vegetation is slowly stripped away until you're standing on the magnificently bleak downs – totally exhilarating.

Poltesco & Carleon Cove
Poltesco Stream has its source all the way up on Goonhilly at Croft Pascoe Pool. It's cut a path down to the sea at Carleon Cove where the pebbly beach creates a natural dam and freshwater pool. The beach has great pebbles – fresh dark green serpentine and a weathered, dark red variety, mottled gabbro and pink Kennack Gneiss, all conveniently polished by the sea. Look out for the *Purple Loosestrife* that grows on the banks of the pool. The Lizard Serpentine Company set up a factory here in 1853, reusing some old fish cellars and the capstan house. A water-powered saw was used to cut and polish serpentine stone, a

Poltesco

fashionable facing for ornate shop fronts, banking halls and wealthy drawing rooms in the City of London. It was a relatively short lived fashion and within 45 years demand had faded away and the factory closed.

Cadgwith Cove

Cadgwith Village

This is a favourite of many visitors. Everything is centred around the small cove. Within 20 metres there's a pub, tea house, gallery, fish shop and a shop with ice creams and gifts. You can buy a necklace or a lobster; a painting or a pint. It's better shopping than Harvey Nichols and after you've shopped yourself to exhaustion you can sit and watch the boats unload their catches on the beach or, sit on the grassy Todden and watch gig boat practice in the bay. The local pub is known throughout West Cornwall for the singing of Cornish songs on a Friday night and there are barbecues on the beach in the summer.

Geology

Just north of **Cadgwith** you cross the fault between the Goonhilly sheet and the Man O'War sheet. Towards **Landewednack** there's a thin coastal strip of schist, Kennack Gneiss & gabbro, which explains the large number of caves & coves carved out by the sea. Most of the valleys on this side of the Lizard are eroded out of Kennack Gneiss, so this is the base of the Goonhilly sheet. Great boulders of it sit in the stream at **Carleon Cove**. The beach here is good for pebbles. There are really 'fresh' dark green serpentine boulders on the beach.

83

Walk 15

Paths onto Goonhilly Downs

Access point

Bray's Cot Pool

Bray's Cot

Prehistoric barrows

Erisey

Prehistoric barrows

Chiverton Croft

Chybarles

Gweal Goose

Chiverton

Tussler's Bridge

Chapel Stile

Crouder's Bridge

Trerise

Cargey Gate

Gwendreath

Parc-an-crouse

Path to Eglos Farm café & Ruan Major Church (ruin)

Kingey

Silver Sands Holiday Park

Gwendreath Holiday Pa

Friar's Lane

Tresaddern

Kuggar

Namparra

Chy Carne

Kennack Sa

Pons Medda

Crowgey Farm

Corgerrick

Kennack Sands Park

Sea Acres Park

Long

Boler Anim Sanct enture

Walk 16
Erisey
5.8km (3½ miles)
2–3 hours

Treal

Treveddon Farm

orner

37

Polstangey Farm

Poltesco Farm

Thorny Cliff

Cavo

Polbre

Little Cove

Todden

Poltesco

Treleague

Mill

Poltesco Lane

Poltesco

Carleon (Poltesco Cove

Black Rock

Serpentine

Ruan Valley

Treleague Crossroads

Friar's Lane

Carleon

Walk 17
Poltesco Stroll
• 1.6km (1 mile)
• 1 hour

St Ruan

Bruggan

Sch

Ruan Minor

SS Highland 1907

Ledgeve

Enys He

St Ruan's Well
Medieval Holy Well

New Road

Steep, narrow road (avoid in summer)

Brandise

Kildown Cov Signal Staff Q (serpentine, dis

Kildown Point

GOONHILLY

Chyheira Farm

Cadgwith

Prazegooth Lane

Terrick The Colt

Huers Hut

Fishing Cove

The Todden

MAN O'WAR 500 million ye rocks that prec creation of th Ocean

Anvoaze

St Grada's Church

Gwavas Vean

Prazegooth

Ynyswidden

Little Cove (Swimming Cove)

Devil's Frying Pan (Collapsed cave)

Dollar Ogo

Chough's Ogo

Carn Barrow

Schist crags & cliffs

Trethvas Farm

Gwavas Farm

Socoa stranded 1906

Serpentine

Polgwidden

Polbarrow Arch

0   0.25km   0.5km   0.75k

¼ mile   ½ n

The Devil's Frying Pan

The Cornish is Hugga Dridgee (Cornish, *ogo* is *cave* and *trig* is *ebb* or *low tide*). It's a cave that has had its roof collapse. This one has been here for at least 400 years. The Lion's Den is a more recent example. Water swirls around the entrance on a high tide.

Erisey Barton

Old farmers will tell you that you can tell the fertility of the land by the quality of the farm buildings. Nowhere is this more true than at Erisey, which is a superb old manor house set in the fertile Poltesco Valley.

St Ruan

The withdrawal of Rome from Britain in AD410 precipitated a period of great population movement in the early Dark Ages. As part of that movement in the C5th and C6th, Christian saints arrived in Cornwall from Ireland and Wales. As they travelled across Cornwall they founded sacred sites, often taking over Iron Age rounds as at Merther Uny, sometimes making an oval *lann* enclosure as at Manaccan and St Anthony. Many Cornish churches now appear to be in odd, isolated places – but it's simply that they were established before towns even existed. St Ruan is a particular favourite on the Lizard. He's said to have lived in a small cell on Goonhilly Downs and to have been magically invulnerable to the wolves who roamed there. In fact, tradition sometimes has him as a werewolf – although this might be a mistranslation, he might simply have been a hairy individual. He was responsible for finally driving the wolves out altogether. Two churches are dedicated to him, Ruan Major, which is now abandoned but within walking distance of Erisey, and the church at Ruan Minor near Cadgwith. His relics were venerated at Ruan Lanihorne.

Above
This barn at Erisey has been faced with blocks of serpentine ashlar in a restrained Georgian classical style. It's actually one of few buildings on the Lizard that uses serpentine as a decorative stone. Undoubtedly the finest building on the Lizard peninsula.

Below
St Ruan's Holy Well near Cadgwith. The structure is probably from the C18th but the site may well date to when St Ruan roamed here, 1,500 years ago.

Walk 18

Landewednack, Bass Point, Housel Bay & Lizard Point

A beautiful bay

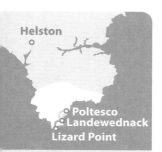

Helston

Poltesco
Landewednack
Lizard Point

BUS
Helston - Lizard Town bus, Lizard Town or Cross Common stops plus Ruan Minor above Cadgwith.

CAR PARKS
National Trust car park at Lizard Point. There's a limited amount of free parking on Lizard Green & about 10 spaces by Landewednack Church.

FOOD & DRINKS
Lizard Town has cafes, a food shop & pub. Housel Bay Hotel does teas & meals.

LOOK OUT FOR...
- Choughs on the cliffs
- *Fringed Rupture-wort* on the coast path by the lighthouse
- Swim at Housel Bay
- Lizard Wireless Station – run by the National Trust & open at peak summer times
- The Lighthouse Centre

We turn the corner from the sheltered east coast cliffs on to the more exposed southern cliffs. The schist cliffs here are more thickly cloaked in plants than the serpentine ever is and their edges are softly bevelled with handsome craggy outcrops – home to the diminutive, rare and celebrated *Fringed Rupture-wort*.

Landewednack Church Cove
The church is thought to have been founded by the monks of Landévennec Abbey in Brittany (the name may be a simple transposition) and dedicated to their patron and abbot, St Winwalloe who we will meet again at Gunwalloe on the west coast of the Lizard.

Bass Point & Lloyds Signal Station
The story of the Lizard in modern times is one bound up with the story of communications – the pioneering development of telegraph, undersea telecom cables and radio are all represented in this one small area. Lizard Signal Station on Bass Point was built in 1872 by the shipping agents Fox & Company of Falmouth (the owners of Glendurgan on the Helford) so that inbound ships could communicate by semaphore flag with the station. When they arrived at Lizard Point ships may have been at sea for months without communication

with their owners. The ship owner could then be telegraphed and would in return relay orders to the captain about which markets were giving the best prices. Approaching Bass Point was itself a major cause of shipwreck

Housel Bay with the handsome schist crags of Pen Olver.

and stranding. In 1883 the operation was taken over by Lloyds of London. The red painted wall by the footpath is a shipping day mark and aligns with the building behind to identify the position of Vrogue Rock. Marconi set up the Lizard Wireless Station in 1901 to experiment with radio messaging. The original huts have been restored by the National Trust and are open in the summer.

The Mosel stops for an excursion

The 1882 story of the *Mosel* is a pleasing antidote to the tales of wreck and misfortune on the Lizard coast. Bound for America with 720 emigrants and crew, she steamed straight into Bass Point in thick fog and went aground directly under the signal station. Fortunately, she lay perfectly upright as if she had docked there on purpose. Passengers and crew disembarked along the bow sprite as if they were on an excursion.

Geology

At Cadgwith we moved onto the third block or sheet of rocks that make up the Lizard. At 500 million years old these rocks all predate the creation of the Rheic Ocean of which the Goonhilly & Crousa sheets are a part. Here pillow lavas have been stretched & deformed by earth movements into glossy blue Landewednack schists. They are shot through with layers of green volcanic ash (*right*) that settled on the sea floor above & between the pillow lavas.

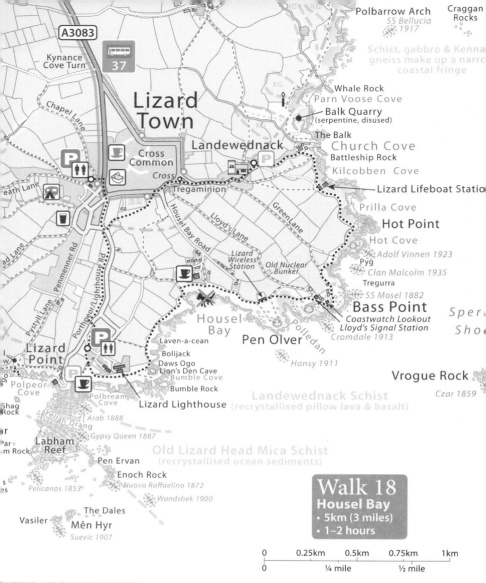

Map labels

A3083

Kynance
Cove Turn

37

Chapel Lane

Lizard
Town

Landewednack

Cross
Common

Cross

Tregaminion

Lloyd's Lane

Green Lane

Housel Bay Road

Lizard
Wireless
Station

Old Nuclear
Bunker

Penmenner Rd

Pystyll Lane

Porthnoor/Lighthouse Rd

Polbarrow Arch
SS Bellucia
1917

Craggan
Rocks

Schist, gabbro & Kenna
gneiss make up a narro
coastal fringe

Whale Rock
Parn Voose Cove

Balk Quarry
(serpentine, disused)

The Balk

Church Cove
Battleship Rock
Kilcobben Cove

Lizard Lifeboat Statio

Prilla Cove

Hot Point

Hot Cove

Adolf Vinnen 1923
Pyg
Clan Malcolm 1935
Tregurra
SS Mosel 1882

Bass Point
Coastwatch Lookout
Lloyd's Signal Station
Cromdale 1913

Sper
Sho

Housel
Bay

Laven-a-cean

Bolijack
Daws Ogo
Lion's Den Cave
Bumble Cove
Bumble Rock

Pen Olver

Polledan

Hansy 1911

Vrogue Rock

Czar 1859

Landewednack Schist
(recrystallised pillow lava & basalt)

Lizard
Point

P

Polpeor
Cove

Polbream
Cove

Shag
Rock

Vellan Drang

Arab 1888

Gypsy Queen 1887

Lizard Lighthouse

Labham
Reef

Pen Ervan

Enoch Rock
Nuovo Raffaelino 1872

Wandsbek 1900

Pelicanos 1853

The Dales

Vasiler

Mên Hyr

Suevic 1907

Old Lizard Head Mica Schist
(recrystallised ocean sediments)

Walk 18
Housel Bay
• 5km (3 miles)
• 1–2 hours

0	0.25km	0.5km	0.75km	1km
0		¼ mile		½ mile

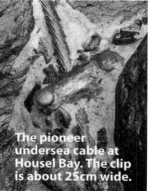

The pioneer undersea cable at Housel Bay. The clip is about 25cm wide.

Housel Bay

To my mind, this is the best of Lizard beauty spots. In 1872 this was the terminal for a pioneer undersea communications cable between the Lizard and Bilbao. The original cable is still clearly visible cut into the cliff face. It only operated for four years before a new cable had to be laid at Kennack Sands because of damage caused by the rocky seabed. I like the way it is fixed back to the cliff using gigantic iron versions of the clips that fasten the telephone cable in your own house.

The Suevic is broken

She ran aground in 1907 on the Mên Hyr rocks in poor visibility. The bow was badly damaged and impaled on the rocks but the rear section, with the engine room and most of the passenger cabins, was undamaged. Her bow was dynamited and, in what must surely rank as one of the most bizarre sights ever to pass up the English Channel, her rear section then steamed in reverse under her own power to Southampton where a new bow was fitted.

Lizard Point & Lighthouse

Sometimes welcomed as a first landfall after a long sea voyage, but all too often grimly surveyed by seamen who knew they were approaching their own graves. The reefs off Lizard Point snake out to sea ready to snare any passing ship that comes too close. At a time when ships navigated by the stars and often hugged the coast for safety, even patchy fog could be fatal. A severe storm could cost hundreds of lives. The lighthouse was built in 1752 to replace a failed private lighthouse built by the Falmouth privateer Sir John Killigrew. Sir John thought he could run a good scam by charging passing shipping for providing the light but he never managed to make it pay. Sir John and his family always lived on the edge of the law. His wife Lady Jane was a notorious pirate.

Flora

The south-facing cliffs & free-draining soils on the schist favour Lusitanian plants like *Fringed Rupture-wort*. It's found only on the British mainland at the Lizard. Dried & taken with wine it was thought to cure rupture or hernia – hence its Latin name *Herniaria ciliolata*. Also said to be efficacious on gonorrhoea & festulous ulcers, especially the sort that are foul & spreading. A big claim for a such a modest little plant. Look out for it on the path below the Lighthouse.

Fringed Rupture-wort

Babington's Leek at Housel Bay

Walk 19

Lizard Point, Pentreath & Kynance Cove

A jewel in a savage setting

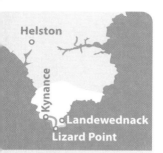

Helston
Kynance
Landewednack
Lizard Point

BUS

Helston - Lizard Town bus, Lizard Town stop or jump off at Kynance Garage & walk across Lizard Downs to Kynance Cove.

PARKING

National Trust car parks at Lizard Point & above Kynance; there's a limited amount of free parking on The Green at Lizard Town.

FOOD & DRINKS

Well provided for in the season with cafes at Kynance Cove, Lizard Point & Lizard Town. Pub & food shops in Lizard Town.

LOOK OUT FOR...

- Choughs all along this coast
- Clovers from Lizard Point to Caerthillian Cove
- Pebbles at Pystyll Ogo
- Kynance Gate prehistoric village
- Serpentine pebbles & cliffs at Kynance

This is by far the most popular stretch of coast on the Lizard and it's full of delights and interest. These serpentine and schist cliffs take a fearful lashing in the winter – there's hardly a shrub, let alone a tree, to be seen. So it's all the more dazzling in the summer, when the turf blossoms with *Harebells*, *Bird's-foot Trefoil*, *Kidney Vetch*, daisies and clovers. Without doubt these are the most colourful cliffs in Cornwall.

Lizard Point

Lizard Point is mentioned as an important landmark on the tin trade route between the Mediterranean and Cornwall by Greek and Roman authors. More recently, it's been a communications hub with the maritime telegraph station at nearby Bass Point. The cafes at Lizard Point are often open in the winter so it's a great place to sit and watch the tail end of a gale blow through. The lifeboat station was sited here in the days when the lifeboats were powered only by oar and raw muscle – this was simply the nearest point to the main wrecking ground. When larger, motorised boats were introduced, the exposed position and lack of water at low tide restricted launching, so a new station was built at Kilcobben Cove.

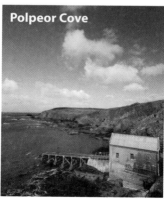

Polpeor Cove

Pystyll Ogo & Pystyll Meadow

The grassy meadow here is the site of one of the most gruesome episodes in the long list of wrecks on the Lizard reefs. *HMS Royal Anne* was a Royal Navy galley, powered by oars as well a sails.

Kynance Cove

She was on her way to protect the West Africa slave trade from pirates when, in November 1721, she sailed into a gale in the Western Approaches. She was driven backwards towards the Lizard finally going aground on the Stags where she disintegrated so rapidly that people were thrown directly from their hammocks into the sea. More than 200 people lost their lives; most are buried in shallow pits on the low cliff and meadow above Pystyll Ogo where the bodies came ashore. Over the following weeks there were reports of stray dogs feasting on the bodies and for many years after that, horrified locals would stone any stray dog they came across. There's a little path down to the beach where, under the small waterfall (Cornish: *Pystyll* is *waterfall*, *ogo* is *cave*) you can pick up beautiful pebbles – mainly basalt, Man O'War Gneiss and Old Lizard Head schists. In the autumn seals give birth in the more secluded caves and choughs also breed here in the summer.

Geology

This corner of the Lizard from Polpeor Cove to Caerthillian Cove is mainly Old Lizard Head schist – deformed sedimentary rocks from about 500 million years ago. The offshore reefs at Lizard Point are Man O'War Gneiss – greatly deformed granites from the Gondwanian plate that drove north to override & destroy the Rheic Ocean.

Flora

The cliffs here are very exposed to gales & are kept closely trimmed by both rabbits & wind. *Spring Squill & Sea Campion* get the show going, followed by a dazzling summer display when the turf blossoms with *Harebells*, *Bird's-foot Trefoil*, *Kidney Vetch*, daisies & clovers. These cliffs are without doubt the most colourful in Cornwall. *Bloody Cranesbill* grows on scree slopes on the path down to Kynance Cove.

Wild Thyme

Thyme Broomrape

Pentreath Beach & Caerthillian Valley

This beach, exposed at low water, has become a little difficult to access because of rock falls on the old path west of Carn Caerthillian. The easiest way to get onto the beach now is to scramble down the low cliffs around Caerthillian Cove. A popular beach with surfers.

Kynance Cove

Idealised by romantic painters and poets in the C18th and C19th, it's a sublime arrangement of untamed and savage nature in a picturesque arrangement of islands, cliffs and sand. Try to arrive when the tide is falling as many of the caves, with their beautiful naturally polished walls, are inaccessible at high water.

Kynance Gate Prehistoric Village

This is a rare chance on the Lizard to walk around a prehistoric settlement. It dates from the Bronze Age about 3,200 years ago and was occupied for three or four hundred years. It was probably a summer settlement as there aren't any fields nearby. The southern group of huts is grouped around a prominent natural outcrop of serpentine with an inclined stone set at its centre – a little reminiscent of the central stone at Boscawen-ûn Circle near Penzance. A later, northern group of five houses are difficult to make out once the summer vegetation has taken hold. An information board at the site has more information. There's a strong visual link with a prominent barrow on the skyline to the northeast. You can walk to it from here.

Kynance Farm

Prehistoric barrow on skyline

Permissive path linking Lizard Downs & Windmill Farm Nature Reserve

Kynance Garage

Grochall Farm

Mile End

If you're arriving by bus you could jump off at Kynance Garage & walk across Lizard Downs

Kissing gate

Kynance Gate
Prehistoric Village

Dead end path

Kynance Brook

Kynance North Valley

Lizard Downs

Kynance South Valley

Goose Curtain Brook

A3083

Kynance Heights

Tor Balk

Lawarnick Pit

Lawarnick Cove

aragus Island

The Devil's Letterbox
Gull Rock

rpentine

The Bishop

Kynance Cove

Lion Rock

Yellow Carn

Holestrow

Enys Vean

Maud 1912
Boiler visible at low tide

Carn Goon

Carn Caerthillian

Kynance Cove Turn

Lizard Town

Chapel Lane

Pentreath Lane

GOONHILLY SHEET

MAN O'WAR SHEET
500 million year old rocks that predate the creation of the Rheic Ocean

Landewednack Schist
(recrystallised pillow lava & basalt)

Old Lizard Head Schists
(recrystallised ocean sediments)

Pentreath Cliff

Pentreath Beach

Caerthillian Cove

Crane Ledges

Holseer Cove

Scathe

Venton Hill Point

Lizard Head Lane

Pystyll Lane

Penmenner Rd

Porthgpeor/Lighthouse Rd

Suffolk 1886

Pystyll Meadow

Lizard Point

Polpeor Cove

Polbre Cove

Old Lizard Head

Xanthus 1841

Quadrant

HMS Royal Anne 1721
Queen Margret 1913

Mulvin

Stags

Man O'War

Clanker Drang

Lead Pool

Pystyll Ogo

Shag Rock

Vellan Drang

Arab 18..

Gypsy

Taylor's Rock
Eltyenburgh 1854

Mên Par
Labham Rock

Labham Reef

Pen

Man of War Gneiss & granite
(Heavily deformed granite rocks from the Gondwanian plate that crashed into Cornwall)

Clidgas Rocks or The Cledges

Pelicanos 1853

Vasiler

The Da..

Mên Hyr

Suevic 1907

Walk 19
Lizard & Kynance
- 7km (4¼ miles)
- 2–3 hours

| 0 | 0.25km | 0.5km | 0.75km | 1km |

| 0 | ¼ mile | ½ mile |

Walks 20 & 21

Predannack, Gew-graze, Vellan Head & Kynance

Black cliffs of the West Coast

BUS

Helston - Lizard Town bus, jump off at Kynance Garage & walk across Lizard Downs to Kynance Cove.

CAR PARKING

National Trust car parks at Predannack Wollas & Kynance Cove.

FOOD & DRINKS

If you're parking at Predannack, there are pasty shops & cafes in Mullion. If you're parking at Kynance, you'll find food shops, cafes & pubs in Lizard Town plus Kynance Cafe right on the beach.

LOOK OUT FOR...

- Cornish choughs on the cliffs
- Orchids in early summer
- Windmill Farm Nature Reserve – you can enter from A3083 (Map7, B1) or from the footpaths on Lizard Downs
- Harebells at Gew-graze valley in summer

A raw and lonely part of the Lizard coast, almost completely set on serpentine bedrock. **The Rill** (Cornish for *cleft*) and **Vellan Head** (Cornish, *melyn* is *yellow* presumably from the prominent yellow and orange lichens here) are the most impressive cliffs on the Lizard. At **Predannack Downs** the heathland merges with the coast showing how the plants of the downs, like the heathers, have their origins in the natural habitat of the cliffs. There's only a single farm on the 5km (3 mile) stretch of coast between **Pentreath Beach** and **Pol Cornick**, a stark reminder of the infertility of serpentine soils.

Predannack Airfield

The airfield was built in 1941 to defend Cornish coastal towns, particularly the important docks at Falmouth. Radar stations already existed at Dry Tree (Goonhilly) and Trelanvean to detect hostile bombers. Coastal Command flew patrols against U-boats operating in the English Channel and the Bay of Biscay from here. Its remote location was ideal for secrecy. Barnes Wallis did work here on the bouncing bomb for the Dambusters raid and later at the height of the Cold War, it was used for jet fighter development. The Royal Navy took over control in 1958 and it's now a busy satellite field for the Royal Navy air station at Culdrose. It's used mainly for training helicopter pilots, practising helicopter based commando assaults and for crash rescue and fire practice. Old

Bloody Cranesbill at Kynance

Gew-graze Cove looking towards the table top flatness of Vellan Head.

jets and helicopters are visible from the footpath that skirts the airfield, they are used for rescue practice. The large mock-up air frame is used for fire practice – when it's in action huge plumes of black smoke can be seen from as far away as Penzance and Falmouth.

Windmill Farm

A large area of Predannack Downs was lost under the runways of the airfield in the 1940s but the peripheral areas of the airfield have been spared and are rich habitats. Cornwall Wildlife Trust have reserves on the north of the airfield at North Predannack Downs, and on the east side of the airfield at Windmill Farm. In one of those beguiling adjacencies that you come across on the Lizard, you can sit watching dragonflies hover in front of you, while Royal Navy helicopters buzz back and forwards overhead. The reserve is farmed to encourage birds and invertebrates and there is a small information centre about Lizard wildlife.

Geology

The serpentine cliffs have a striking tabletop flatness. Stand on top of Kynance Cliff today & you're 70m (230ft) above sea level – but 25 million years ago you would be standing at the bottom of a shallow sea. It's the sea that has planed the serpentine flat & as it's very resistant to erosion, little has changed since apart from it being pushed upwards by earth movements. At Crousa Downs near Coverack, which is 30m (100ft) higher still, there are deposits of rounded sea pebbles stranded on top of the downs.

Flora.

There's an unusual plant survival on the valley sides – *Prostrate Juniper*. It's a plant mainly of dry mountainous places, both sub-arctic & Mediterranean. It may have grown here at the end of the last glacial period 15,000 years ago & has managed to cling on ever since. The rocky slopes must replicate in some way its favoured habitat. It's struggling to keep going though. There are about a dozen plants left & most have to be protected from cattle by electric fences.

Harebell

Yellow Bartisa at Windmill Farm

Soapy Cove & Gew-graze Valley

The valley that curves to the sea from Kynance Farm is typical of the serpentine landscape. There's hardly a plant more than knee high. It's all the more eye-catching when the valley path is sprinkled with the nodding heads of Harebells in the late summer. On the north side of the cove is the largest steatite or soapstone quarry on the Lizard. The start of the C18th saw a fashion, verging on mania, for imported Chinese porcelain. The method of manufacture was a well kept secret in China but entrepreneurs here, and in Europe, took on the search for materials that would replicate porcelain's thin, strong and semi-transparent nature. From about 1750 white crumbly talc or soapstone was quarried here and from smaller quarries at Pentreath and Mullion Cove for use in the industry. If you rub any piece of serpentine with your fingers, you will feel the soapy or greasy texture of the rock – this is why the serpentine blocks used in stiles are slippery after rain.

Rill Cove

Spanish silver coins and silver bars from an unnamed wreck of 1618 have been recovered from Rill Cove. The wreck was discovered almost by accident because it's actually overlain by another wreck, the trawler *Kerris Reed* which was lost here in 1968. Sometimes it looks as if ships were queuing up to be wrecked on the Lizard.

The cackling call of Cornish Chough can be heard all along this coast

Teneriffe Farm

nnack
nor

dannack
ollas

Windyridge
Farm

Walk 21
Vellan Head
• 4km (2½ miles)
• 1–2 hours

*Predannack
Downs*

Predannack Airfield
Training area for helicopters
from RNAS Culdrose
(No admittance)

*Lower
Predannack
Downs*

ove

ur Cove

*This path is
invariably
boggy & wet*

*To get to Kynance
take the well made
farm track opposite
the red & white signs*

*Old fighter jets &
helicopters used
for rescue practice*

Dog Brook

*Dragonfly
ponds*

*Nature
Trails*

*Wetland
boardwalks*

Windmill Farm
Nature Reserve

Pol Cornick
Velvet
Rock

George's
Cove

ntine

lan
ad

*Stromboli
1878*

Pengersick

Gersick-an-zawn

Ogo Pons
Gew-graze
(Soapy Cove)

Pigeon Ogo

*Old Quarry
(soap rock/
steatite)*

**Kynance
Farm**

*Prehistoric
barrow on
skyline*

*Kissing
gate*

*Access
point*

Pe
linki
&
N

Kynance

Kynance Gate
Prehistoric Village

*Dead
end
path*

Kynance Brook

Kynance
North Valley

The Horse

The Pound

Kynance Cliff

*Firebreaks
& rough
tracks*

The Rill

Rill Point

Rill Ledges

*Abernyte
1898*

Rill
Cove

Walk 20
The Rill & back
• 3km (2 miles)
• 1–2 hours

Lawarnick
Pit

Lawarnick
Cove

Asparagus Island
The Devil's Letterbox
Gull Rock

Serpentine

Kynance
Heights

Tor Balk

Walk 19

Pentr

Kynance
Cove

The Bishop

Lion Rock

Yellow
Carn   Hole

Enys
Vean

*Maud 1912
Boiler visible at low*

GOONHILLY BLOCK

MAN O'WAR BLOCK
500 million year old rocks that predate
the creation of the Rheic Ocean

| 0 | 0.25km | 0.5km | 0.75km | 1km |

| 0 | ¼ mile | ½ mile |

Walk 22

Predannack, Ogo-dour, Mullion Cove & Polurrian

Orchids & sea gulls

BUS
Helston - Lizard Town bus, Mullion Cricket Club stop, 1.2km (¾ mile) from Mullion Cove.

CAR PARKING
Large public car parks at Mullion Cove & Poldhu. National Trust car park at Predannack Wollas.

FOOD & DRINKS
Pasties, food shops, cafes & pub in Mullion & cafe at Mullion Meadows. Polurrian has a beach cafe.

LOOK OUT FOR...
• Sea birds on Mullion Island and The Vro – bring some binoculars
• Take the bus to Lizard Town & take a day to walk from Lizard Point to Mullion where you can pick the bus up once more. It's about 11km (7 miles) on the coast path – a bit less if you shortcut across some of the headlands.
• Gift shops at Mullion Meadows

This is the final section before we leave the Lizard rocks behind us at **Polurrian**. At **Ogo-dour Cove** (Cornish, *ogo* is *cave*, *dour* is *water*) the cliffs change and soften. The heath-covered serpentine cliffs are replaced by the grassy slopes of schist at **Predannack Head** and they are grazed by herds of Shetland ponies. At **Predannack Morva** the path briefly drops down to a small stream and then rises dramatically back onto the serpentine of **Mullion Cliff** – the highest on the Lizard. The black serpentine cliffs make a final brief reappearance above **Porth Pyg** (Cornish, *pyk* for *beak* or *spout*) before descending towards Mullion Cove and Polurrian.

Mullion Cove
Rising sea levels and a century of storms and gales have taken their toll on the harbour and it's been decided that any major damage to the quay will not be repaired. A similar quay at Lamorna on the Land's End peninsula has already been reclaimed by the sea. Occasional boat trips leave from the harbour in the summer to view the coastline and watch the birds and seals on Mullion Island. A small tunnel runs from the harbour through the cliff to the beach at Porth Pyg.

Mullion Island

The Vro & Mullion Island
The island is a home to colonies of seabirds. Kittiwake, cormorant, razorbill, guillemot, black backed gulls and peregrine falcon all breed here. Seals haul themselves out onto the rocks to sunbathe.

Ogo-dour Cove

Mullion Village

This is the largest village on the peninsula and it's a thriving local community based around farming, tourism and some fishing from Mullion Cove. The large secondary school serves the whole of the Lizard peninsula. The centre has shops and galleries. It sits astride the Lizard boundary with one foot on the serpentine and one foot on the slate. It's only a short walk from the village to Mullion Cove or Polurrian and on to the coastal footpaths.

Polurrian

A huge sandy beach popular with surfers and families. Just north of **Pedn-y-ke** there's a 10 metre wide zone of shattered and crushed rock in the cliff. This is where the Lizard rocks have been faulted against the slates of Cornwall and where the Lizard block has been thrust up many kilometres from the Earth's interior.

Geology.

Predannack Head is an island of Traboe schist (deformed cumulate & gabbro) surrounded by & infolded with the serpentine. It's the Goonhilly sheet's equivalent of the transition zone near the Moho, which we saw at Coverack. **Mullion Island** is a raft of well-preserved pillow lava. It's probably part of the Roseland Breccia (there must be a fault running between the island & the cliffs). Rafts of pillow lava this size also occur inland in the Meneage. At **Polurrian** there is a sharp fault at Pedn-y-ke which marks the end of the Lizard rocks.

Flora

Our friend of the festiferous sores, *Fringed Rupture-wort* that was visible below Lizard Lighthouse & on crags of schist at Pentreath makes a reappearance here along with clovers. In April the cliffs are covered in a delightful blue haze of *Spring Squill*. Also look out for *Green Winged Orchids*. Natural England and the National Trust maintain the cliff and heath habitat by grazing wild ponies and Soay sheep to keep down the grasses and increase the diversity of wild plants.

Mullion Cove

Sea Aster

Sheep's-bit

Guillemot

Razorbill

Kittiwake

Black backed gull

Cormorant

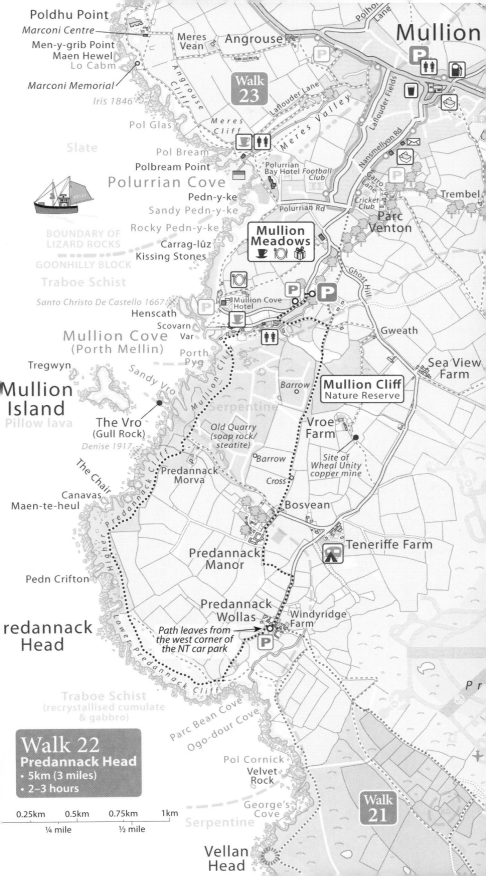

Poldhu Point
Marconi Centre
Men-y-grib Point
Maen Hewel
Lo Cabm
Marconi Memorial
Iris 1846

Meres Vean
Angrouse
Mullion

Walk 23

Angrouse Cliff

Meres Cliff

Laffouder Lane

Meres Valley

Laffouder Fields

Nansmellyon Rd

Pol Glas

Slate

Pol Bream

Polbream Point

Polurrian Cove

Pedn-y-ke
Sandy Pedn-y-ke
Rocky Pedn-y-ke
Carrag-lûz
Kissing Stones

Polurrian Bay Hotel
Football Club

Polurrian Rd

Garro Lane

Cricket Club

Trembel

Parc Venton

BOUNDARY OF LIZARD ROCKS
GOONHILLY BLOCK

Traboe Schist

Santo Christo De Castello 1667

Henscath
Scovarn Var

Mullion Cove
(Porth Mellin)

Porth Pyg

Mullion Meadows

Mullion Cove Hotel

Ghost Hill

Gweath

Sea View Farm

Tregwyn

Mullion Island

Pillow lava

Sandy Vro

The Vro
(Gull Rock)

Denise 1917

Mullion Cliff

Serpentine

Barrow

Old Quarry
(soap rock/
steatite)

Mullion Cliff
Nature Reserve

Vroe Farm

Site of
Wheal Unity
copper mine

The Chair

Predannack Morva

Barrow

Cross

Bosvean

Canavas
Maen-te-heul

Higher Predannack Cliff

Predannack Manor

Teneriffe Farm

Pedn Crifton

Predannack Wollas

Windyridge Farm

Lower Predannack Cliff

redannack Head

*Path leaves from
the west corner of
the NT car park*

Traboe Schist
(recrystallised cumulate
& gabbro)

Parc Bean Cove

Ogo-dour Cove

Pr

Walk 22
Predannack Head
• 5km (3 miles)
• 2–3 hours

Pol Cornick
Velvet Rock

George's Cove

Serpentine

Walk 21

0.25km   0.5km   0.75km   1km
¼ mile   ½ mile

Vellan Head

Looking over Jangye-ryn beach from Castle Mound at Gunwalloe.
The cliffs are typical of slate – a far cry from The Rill & Vellan Head.

3. Porthleven & the west coast
Poldhu to Porthleven & Trewavas Head

POLURRIAN MARKS THE ABRUPT END of the rare and unusual rocks of the Lizard and the start of a softer coastline of small inlets and pebbly coves backed by crumbly slate cliffs. **Church Cove** at **Gunwalloe** is one of those places where happy family days are made. It's got all the ingredients needed – an ancient church built implausibly close to the beach, sand dunes to run and hide in and a stream to dam. Stir in legends of wrecked Spanish galleons spilling Aztec treasure chests into **Dollar Cove** and you have a thrilling mix. Even today, silver coins occasionally turn up on the beach. Searching the pebbles for Montezuma's treasure will keep the whole family busy for hours.

Further along the coast and past the cliffs at **Halzephron** – *Hell's Cliffs* in Cornish – the 4 kilometres of flint pebbles that make up Loe Bar is an ideal place for a blowy walk followed by a pint at the Halzephron Inn. The sand and shingle has blocked the estuary of the River Cober to create **Loe Pool**. The wooded walks around the pool are a rare treat in wind blasted West Cornwall where trees are sparse. Car parks dot the banks and creeks so you can tailor the length of the walk to suit your mood.

On a coast as fearsome and sparsely populated as this one, the harbour at **Porthleven** is a rare haven. It's busy and full of life. The harbour quays once stacked with pit props for local mines and kegs of china clay are now busy with visitors to the craft shops, restaurants and artists' studios. It's also become a haven for foodies, especially for its locally caught smoked fish. This book ends on the granite headland of **Trewavas Head**. At **Rinsey Cove** you get a real flavour of the granite coves to come on the Land's End peninsula.

GETTING AROUND

BUS

The Helston - Lizard Town service will get you within walking distance of the main beaches at Poldhu & Polurrian. Jump off at Mullion Golf Course for Church Cove, Gunwalloe. Jump off at Cury Church & walk across the top of Gunwalloe Marsh to Halzephron.
The Helston - Penzance service will get you to Loe Bar (Penrose Hill stop) & to Porthleven.

Porthleven

PLACES TO VISIT

- Helston Folk Museum. Eccentric collection of all sorts from prehistory to 1960s cookers & toasters, check opening times before you visit
- Flambards Fun Fair
- Back bar of the Blue Anchor in Helston or front bar of the Ship Inn at Porthleven

West Coast of the Lizard

Poldhu, Gunwalloe Cove, Jangye-ryn & Halzephron

The church of the storms

Helston
Loe Pool
Gunwalloe
Mullion

Lizard Point

BUS

Helston - Lizard Town bus, Mullion Golf Club or Poldhu stops & then 10min walk to Church Cove. If you're doing the walk behind Gunwalloe Marsh jump off at Cury Church – you can pick the bus up again at Poldhu.

CAR PARKING

There's a large National Trust car park behind the beach at Gunwalloe. Small car park at top of the lane from Poldhu to Carrag-a-pilez Cliff. Space for 2 or 3 cars above Halzephron Cove on the remains of the old road (the rest has disappeared over the cliff).

FOOD & DRINKS

Beach shop at Gunwalloe in the summer for take away teas. Barefoot Cafe at Halzephron House, Halzephron Inn at Chyanvounder.

LOOK OUT FOR...
- Treasure on the beach at Jangye-ryn
- Marconi Centre

The Lizard rocks give way to the glorious beaches at Polurrian, **Poldhu** and **Gunwalloe**. How very different from the brooding black cliffs of Mullion and Kynance. The cliff walk from **Poldhu** to **Gunwalloe** takes just 10 minutes but to go by car it's an 11km (7 mile) journey as the road veers inland to avoid **Gunwalloe Marsh.** We've picked a less used walk from **Cury Church Town** that passes across the top of Gunwalloe Marsh to the **Halzephron Inn** and then back along the coast to Poldhu. Although the start and finish points are both on the Poldhu to Cury road and quite close together, we haven't shown this as a circular walk because the road is narrow and busy.

Jangye-ryn & Church Cove, Gunwalloe

At least two treasure ships have been lost here. The *Schiedam* was wrecked on Jangye-ryn beach in 1684. Dozens of cannons lie on the sea bed just offshore and pewter spoons, candlesticks and coins have all been found here (Jangye-ryn is often called Dollar Cove). An unknown treasure ship spilled gold and silver coins into the cleft of a different Dollar Cove on Castle Mound and silver pieces-of-eight turn up every now and then, dislodged by storms from the rocky gullies.

Church Cove Gunwalloe

Poldhu

Poldhu & Marconi

A very popular surfing and family beach. In December 1901 the first radio signal to cross the Atlantic was sent from Poldhu to Newfoundland starting the radio revolution. The masts have long since gone, Goonhilly is the now the modern communication centre. You can still wander around the site and there's an exhibition at the Marconi Centre.

The Marconi radio station at Poldhu

Geology

The low cliffs of **Jangye-ryn** & **Porthleven** illustrate what geologists call *crustal shortening*, which not only sounds unpleasant but looks painful too. Mud laid down in horizontal layers has been squeezed into contorted folds by earth movements caused by the thrusting of the Lizard.

Above
The *Church of the Storms*
at Gunwalloe Cove. The
church is from the second
great period of Medieval
building in the C14th &
C15th & is said to contain
wood salvaged from the
wreck of the *San Antonio*
in 1527.
Below
At least two treasure ships
have been wrecked at
Gunwalloe. Every now
& then Spanish pieces-
of-eight turn up on the
beach.

St Winwalloe's Church

A small, simple and beautiful Cornish church
known over time as the *Church of the Storms*.
It's tucked behind the small headland known
as Castle Mound and has been threatened
many times by the sea. St Winwalloe was born
in Brittany about AD460 to the Welsh princess
Gwen Teirbron or Gwen the triple-breasted
because she had one breast for each of her
three sons. His father was Fracan, a Celtic
prince, and he grew up as a pupil of Saint
Budoc of Budock Vean and Budock Water
near Falmouth. He founded the monastery of
Landévennec near Brest in AD485 and is revered at
Landewednack near Lizard Town (possibly a straight
transposition of the Breton name). There were very
close links between Cornwall and Brittany at this time
because of a great migration from Cornwall following
a plague (or the Saxon invasions). It may be that they
were even part of a single kingdom. The links were
so deeply rooted that even in the early Medieval
period Breton would be more understandable to a
Cornishman than English.

Halzephron & the loss of the James & Rebecca

The transport ship *James & Rebecca* was returning from
South America with a squadron of Light Dragoons in
November 1807 when she ran into trouble below the
high cliffs of Halzephron (Cornish: *als* for *cliff*, *yfarn*
for *hells*). She fired her guns to attract assistance but
rescuers struggled to get to her because of the height
of the cliffs. During the night 100 of the 200 people
on board had been hauled up the cliff to safety but by
mid morning her hull gave way and all the remaining
passengers and crew were thrown into the sea where
41 drowned. They're buried on the cliff top.

Park Be
Fabe
Halzep
Co
Ja
Rebe
41 d

Pedngw

Folded s
in cli

Walk 23
Gunwalloe Marsh
- 5.5km (3½ miles)
- 2–3 hours

| 0 | 0.25km | 0.5km | 0.75km | 1km |
| 0 | ¼ mile | | ½ mile | |

Berepper

Polgrean Farm

Gunwalloe

Millewarne

Anhay Farm

warne Mill

Chyanvounder

Burgess (abandoned)

Trevergy Farm

Transingove

Trenoweth Farm

Chepy (abandoned)

Colvenno Farm

Sowanna Farm

Cury White C

Halzephron House

Toll

Hingey Farm

Chymder

Cury Churchtown

Nanfan Farm

Gwills

Busy & narrow road with no pavement

Winnianton

Beachshop

Clubhouse

Mullion Golf Course

Towan Cottages

Priske

gye-ryn hing or ar Cove) astle Mound Dollar Cove

Church Cove (unwalloe Beach)
Carrag-a-pilez reef
SS Grip 1887
San Salvador 1669
Monkheer Meester Van Der Wall Putteshock 1867

The Towans

Round Barrows

37

Polhorman Farm

Newton Farm

Poldhu Cove

Poldhu Point
Marconi Centre
Men-y-grib Point
Maen Hewel
Lo Cabm

Marconi Memorial
Iris 1846

Meres Vean

Angrouse

Mullion

Polhorman Lane

Pol Glas

Meres Cliff

Angrouse Cliff

Lanouder Lane

Meres Valley

Lanouder Fields

Nansmellyon Rd

Slate

Pol Bream
Polbream Point

Polurrian Cove
Pedn-y-ke
Sandy Pedn-y-ke
Rocky Pedn-y-ke
Carrag-lûz
Kissing Stones

Polurrian Bay Hotel

Football Club

Polurrian Rd

Garfo Lane

Cricket Club

Parc Venton

Trembe

BOUNDARY OF LIZARD ROCKS
GOONHILLY BLOCK

Traboe Schist

Mullion Meadows

Santo Christo De Castello 1667

Mullion Cove Hotel

Walk 24

Loe Bar, Loe Pool & Helston

An estuary imprisoned

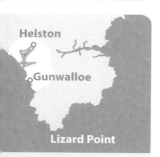

BUS
Helston - Penzance bus, Penrose Hill stop or Boating Lake stop at the bottom of Helston. If you're coming from other parts of the Lizard jump off at **Coinage Hall Street** (Blue Anchor) in Helston where you can pick up a pasty & walk down to the Boating Lake.

CAR PARKING
National Trust car parks are dotted around Loe Pool.

FOOD & DRINKS
Nothing on the walk itself but you can pick up sandwiches & pasties in Helston & Porthleven.

LOOK OUT FOR...
- Helston Folk Museum
- Yellow Horned Poppy on the bar
- The waves after a gale
- Hire a pedalo on Helston Boating Lake

BEWARE
Even on a calm day at Loe Bar large waves can take the unwary by surprise. Don't be tempted to even paddle or swim in the sea here.

The National Trust have made the area around **Loe Pool** (Cornish: *loe* is *logh* or *lake*) very open and accessible. You can walk around the whole of Loe Pool in a day but most people choose to walk smaller sections starting at one of the car parks dotted around the edge. The west side is the most popular as it follows a bumpy driveway from **Helston Boating Lake** to **Bar Lodge**. It's good enough for cycling and for pushing a buggy. A quieter, less used footpath follows the eastern side, but is only suitable for walkers.

Helston
By modern-day standards Helston is off the beaten track. Like Penzance it has many fine Georgian buildings which show the wealth that flowed through the town from the tin and copper mines. It's the nearest large town to the Lizard and has a wider range of facilities than can be found in Mullion or at Lizard Town. This includes the excellent facility of the Blue Anchor in Coinagehall Street. It brews its own beer – the famous *Spingo*, reputedly only sold in half pint measures to strangers in case it leaves them speechless and trembling with its potency. Helston's

Yellow Horned Poppy

Folk Museum is a little gem. It's housed in the old butter market and the walls are lined with old carts, a huge timber cider press and it's packed full of local archaeological finds and a great collection of 1960s cookers and radios.

Looking over Loe Bar to Loe Pool. The victims of the Anson were buried close to the memorial 'without coffin, shroud or ceremony'.

HMS Anson is wrecked

In December 1807 *HMS Anson* ran for cover into Mount's Bay and let out her anchor in the hope of riding out the storm. Her cable parted and she was picked up by the huge waves that fall on Loe Bar and dumped on the shingle, immediately breaking her back. The mast made a gangway of sorts and some of the crew made it to safety but 120 were lost, drowning close to shore in front of hundreds of onlookers who could hear their screams for help but were powerless to save them. Henry Trengrouse, who witnessed this horror, vowed to find a way to prevent disasters like the Anson recurring. His idea was to fire a rocket apparatus from the cliff or beach which would carry a line onto the stricken ship. The crew could then be brought ashore by a chair and pulley system. Known as the Rocket, it saved many hundreds of lives but has been superseded by rescue helicopters from Culdrose.

Flora of shingle

Shingle beach is a rare habitat in Cornwall. *Yellow Horned Poppy* (left) is one of the most beautiful of seaside plants. It grows on the back of the bar near the outfall. The roots of *Sea Holly* (below) were once collected & candied for sale at fairs as an aphrodisiac.

Sea Holly

Flora of shingle

Cabbages, like children, are always happy at the seaside. *Sea Kale* is a very handsome and architectural plant & always attracts the attention of children on the beach.

Down on the strand line you'll often find *Sea Rocket* – another member of the cabbage family. Its seeds are dispersed by the waves & in some years there are hundreds of plants in a single locality, but in the next year there will be none. It does well if winter storms have piled up seaweed on the strand line.

Sea Rocket

Sea Kale

SS Tripolitania 1913. The captain drove her onto Loe Bar to save the crew. She was broken up for scrap.

Loe Bar

In bad weather waves fall on Loe Bar with tremendous force – it's a great sight. The bar drops very steeply below the water so there's nothing to slow the waves down as they roll from the deep water in Mount's Bay to building and breaking on the bar. You can actually feel the vibrations through the shingle 100 metres from the sea's edge. When sailing ships were driven into Mount's Bay by a southwesterly storm they had little hope of getting out. All they could do was pay out as many anchors as possible and hope to ride out the storm before the anchors dragged or separated. Many captains, aware that they couldn't avoid being wrecked, actually chose to head for Loe Beach in preference to being driven under the high cliffs of Halzephron. At least they had a chance of rescue on Loe Bar. There are so many wrecks off Loe Bar, it's said that if the tide went right out you could walk from Porthleven Sands to Gunwalloe Fishing Cove without even touching the seabed.

Helston

St Johns · Mus
Cinema
Wendro

St Elvan

Lanner Vean

🅿 🅿 Blue Anchor
Meneage Street

Boating Lake

Porthleven Road

🅿 A394

Children's Play Park

2, 2A

Penventon

Venton Vedra

B3304

Nansloe Manor

Lower Nansloe

Nansloe Farm

He Ho (minor not

Higher Lanner

Loe Valley

Lower Lanner

Loe Marsh

Nanswidden

Hill 🅿

Helston Lodge

A3083

Penrose House

Bird Hide

The Loe

Degibna

Little Goonhus

Higher Penrose

Penrose Mine (ad, disused)

Degibna Wood

🅿 Chapel

Higher Pentire

Hig Goonh

🅿

Muddy path

Wheal Rose Mine (Lead, disused)

Lower Goonhusband

D

Bar Lodge

Loe Pool

Lower Pentire

Tangies

Vellin-gluz Rocks

Outfall

Carminowe Creek

Little Nanspean

Anson 1781

Bar Sands

Nanspean

Loe Bar

Tripolitania 1912

Anson Memorial

🅿

Clies Farm

Chyvarloe

Berepper

Walk 24
Loe Pool & Bar
• 8.7km (5½ miles)
• 3½ hours

Berepper Cross

Gunwalloe

0.25km   0.5km   0.75km   1km

¼ mile   ½ mile

Porthleven. In a severe storm, waves will break onto the Institute clock tower.

Porthleven to Trewavas & Rinsey Cove

A foretaste of the granite kingdom

The Land's End peninsula has been visible across Mounts Bay all the way from Lizard Point and this book ends on the granite cliffs of **Trewavas Head** and **Rinsey Cove**, with a foretaste of what's to come in our *Land's End Guidebook*.

Porthleven

Porthleven seems an unpromising site for a harbour with its narrow and exposed entrance, but on this coast where shelter is absent and there are no safe anchorages, the granite breakwaters are like soft welcoming arms. One of the motivations for building the harbour was to provide safety for sailing ships driven into Mount's Bay by southwesterly gales. They had little option but to drop anchor and hope to ride out the storm, a strategy that frequently proved fatal. As a last resort some ships would even try and shelter behind Mullion Island, but a more desperate and dangerous anchorage is difficult to imagine.

As well as offering much needed shelter, the close proximity of china clay pits and tin mines enabled the harbour to prosper. Timber and coal were imported for the lead, silver and tin mines nearby and china clay, tin ore and pilchards were exported. A small fishing fleet is still active in the summer. Most of the catch is landed on the other side of Mount's Bay at Newlyn Market but fresh fish is always readily available in the shops, restaurants and pubs around the harbour. Craft shops and artists' studios have taken over the old sail lofts and warehouses. Potters and willow weavers have joined the long-established art community to make Porthleven one of the most enjoyable places to visit in West Cornwall.

BUS

Porthleven is served by the Helston - Penzance bus. Rinsey is a 1.5km (1 mile) walk from the Lion & Lamb stop at Ashton along Rinsey Lane or a 4.5km (2¾ miles) cliff walk from Porthleven.

CAR PARKING

National Trust car park above Rinsey Cove (keep to the right as you drive through Rinsey hamlet).

FOOD & DRINKS

Pubs, cafes & restaurants in Porthleven, plus the Lion & Lamb at Ashton & Queens Arms at Breage (both on A394). You can pick up sandwiches & pasties in Porthleven.

LOOK OUT FOR...

- Boat trips – look for the boards around the harbour
- Rinsey Pool – a natural swimming pool west of Trewavas Head
- The mines on Trewavas Head are as dramatic as the Crowns Mine near Botallack

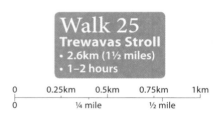

Walk 25
Trewavas Stroll
- 2.6km (1½ miles)
- 1–2 hours

```
0        0.25km      0.5km      0.75km     1km
0              ¼ mile           ½ mile
```

Trewavas Head

This small dome of granite is an outlier of the main Carnmenellis boss that outcrops north of the Helford River and is visible at Merther Uny. Wherever there is granite, there are mines. The lead and silver mines of Wheal Penrose and Wheal Rose sit above Porthleven Sands. On Trewavas Head the engine houses of Trewavas Mine perch on the cliff edge. The shafts run down the cliff face to serve galleries that extend out under the seabed to the lodes of tin and copper. They are as impressive as the famous Crowns Mines at Botallack near Land's End and a provide a suitably dramatic place to end this book.

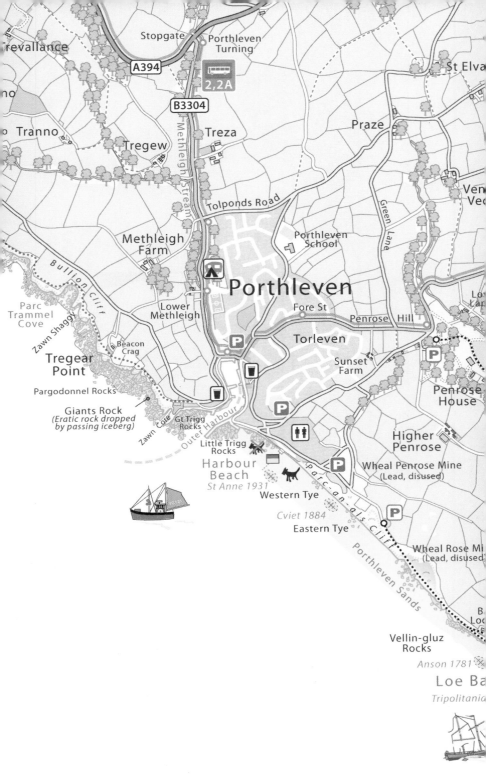

revallance

Stopgate

Porthleven Turning

A394

2,2A

B3304

Tranno

Tregew

Treza

Praze

St Elva

Ven Ved

Tolponds Road

Methleigh Farm

Porthleven School

Green Lane

Lo Lar

Porthleven

Bullion Cliff

Lower Methleigh

Fore St

Penrose Hill

Torleven

Parc Trammel Cove

Beacon Crag

Sunset Farm

Penrose House

Zawn Shaggy

Tregear Point

Pargodonnel Rocks

Giants Rock
*(Eratic rock dropped
by passing iceberg)*

Zawn Cove

Gt Trigg Rocks

Outer Harbour

Little Trigg Rocks

Harbour Beach
St Anne 1931

Higher Penrose

Wheal Penrose Mine
(Lead, disused)

Parc-an-als Cliff

Western Tye

Cviet 1884

Eastern Tye

Wheal Rose Mi
(Lead, disused)

Porthleven Sands

B Loc

Vellin-gluz Rocks

Anson 1781

Loe Ba

Tripolitania

The old copper mines on the granite cliffs of Trewavas Head. In the background horizontal sheets of granite have invaded the overlying slates.

Beach Guide
Treats & favourite things to do
Activities & places to visit
Area Maps
Walks in this book

Helpful information

Lizard beaches

Church Cove, Gunwalloe

The best beaches on the Lizard like **Gunwalloe** (Church Cove), **Poldhu**, **Polurrian** and **Kynance** are on a short stretch of the west coast around Mullion. They have golden sand & are the most likely to have surf. The beaches on the more sheltered east coast tend to be more pebbly but they can be gloriously empty such as **Godrevy Cove** near St Keverne. The exception to this rule is the wonderful family beach at **Kennack Sands**. Many beaches all but disappear at high tide – we've marked them with ≈ so you'll need to check out the tide times.

Beach Guide
Times of high & low water
The Lizard

Beaches
Facilities
Transport links
Times of high & low tide £2

Guide to symbols

▭ Lifeguards in summer
✗ No dogs in summer (some beaches allow dogs after 7pm & before 7am – check at **visitcornwall.com**
Ⓟ Parking nearby
♦ Good for families
🚌 2 On bus route
☕ Cup of tea nearby
🏄 Good for surf dudes
♦ Toilets nearby
⛵ Water activities
≈ Covered at high water

Rinsey Cove ≈ (Porthcew)
Back to nature
Lovely beach northwest of Porthleven. Take Rinsey turning off A394 (Helston–Penzance road) at Ashton or, take minor road that winds up past the Ship Inn in Porthleven. 10min (steep) walk down cliff from National Trust car park at Rinsey. Slightly awkward climb down rocks to beach (climb down facing the rock). Covered at high water. Rinsey Pool, just up coast and a scramble down the cliff, is a natural plunge pool.
Ⓟ 🏄
(Map 1,A2)

Porthleven Harbour Beach
Sandy beach just outside the harbour breakwater. Strong waves – beware rip tides at low water.
▭ ✗ (Dogs OK east of lifeguard hut & steps) All facilities in Porthleven.
🚌 **Helston - Penzance**
(Map 1,C3)

Loe Bar
Don't swim here
A very dangerous, steeply shelving beach with very powerful offshore currents. It looks tempting but don't be fooled.

Gunwalloe Church Cove & Jangye-ryn (Dollar or Fishing Cove)
Perfect for families
Plenty of sand at Church Cove even at high water with a stream & sand dunes for small children to play in. Small beach cafe sells refreshments & pasties. Search for Spanish treasure from a wrecked ship at Dollar Cove. Large NT car park above the beach.
▭ ✗ (OK at Jangye-ryn)
Ⓟ ♦ ⛵🏄 ♦
🚌 **Helston - Lizard Town**
Poldhu or Mullion Golf Club stops & then 10min walk over the dunes/golf course.
(Map 4,B2)

Poldhu

Poldhu Cove ≈

Great for families & surfers

Popular, large sandy beach with sit down cafe (open all year) & large car park.

🚌 **Helston - Lizard Town** (Map 4,B2)

Polurrian Cove ≈

Good for families

Popular, large sandy beach. Nearest parking is in Mullion Village about 10mins walk. Seasonal beach cafe.

🚌 **Helston - Lizard Town** Mullion Cricket Club stop then 10/15min walk. **(Map 4,B3)**

Mullion Cove (Porth Pyg) ≈

A dramatic setting

In recent years there has been very little sand here but if you're lucky there will be a wide expanse of sand exposed for a few hours each side of low tide. Accessible via tunnel from Mullion Cove. Not busy. Dramatic setting against the black serpentine

cliffs. Car park & toilets 5min above Mullion Cove harbour.

🚌 **Helston - Lizard Town** Mullion Cricket Club stop then 10/15min walk to Mullion Cove. **(Map 4,B4)**

Kynance Cove ≈

A romantic setting

A sandy beach with numerous islands & caves to explore. Park in National Trust car park 10min walk above the cove. Ice creams & loos at car park, cafe & loos above beach. Car park quickly fills during school summer holidays & bank holidays.

🚌 **Helston–Lizard Town** Lizard Green stop then 20/25min walk over cliffs or jump off at Kynance Garage and 20min walk over Lizard Downs. **(Map 7,B3)**

Pentreath Beach ≈

Far from the madding crowd

Glorious sandy beach exposed at low water. Unfortunately, the old path from Carn Caerthillian has become dangerous & it doesn't look like access will be possible any time soon from there. Other paths (for the sure footed) go down the low cliffs to the south. Kids love the old boiler stuck in the sand at the north end of the beach. Good surfing. No Facilities.

Ⓟ Just before Carn Goon 🏊

🚌 **Helston–Lizard Town** Lizard Green stop then 15/20mins walk over cliffs. **Map 7,B3**

Polurrian

Lizard beaches

Housel Bay

Housel Bay
Small & perfect
Small beach at foot of cliffs. Housel Bay Hotel above provides bar snacks & meals. Park above Lizard Point then 1km walk along cliff path. Really beautiful bay to swim in – lots of rocks & small islands to explore & jump off. Good place for basking sharks.

Helston - Lizard Town
Tregaminion or Lizard Green stops then 15min walk.
Map 7,C3

Cadgwith Little/Swimming Cove
Tiny, sheltered beach. Pub, toilet & shops nearby. Large car park 5min walk above Cadgwith Cove. No sand at HW but you can still swim off the rocks.

Helston - Lizard Town
Ruan Minor stop, steep, 20min walk down to Cadgwith.
Map 7,D2

Kennack Sands
Perfect family beach
Golden sand, streams & rock pools. Large car park, cafe, shop & toilets.
(but dogs OK on Eastern Beach)

Helston - Lizard Town
Kuggar stop, then 10/15min walk down road.
Map 5,C4

Lankidden Cove
Back to Nature 1
Unofficial naturist beach. Steep & slightly tricky descent from cliff path. No facilities.

Helston - Lizard Town
Kuggar stop, then 10/15min walk down road to Kennack Sands, 30min along coast.
Map 5,D4

Kennack Sands

Downas Cove
Back to Nature 2
Sand uncovered for an hour or two each side of low water only. An 'off the beaten track' beauty spot.
Map 6,A4

Coverack, Mears Beach
Popular little beach with locals. 15min walk along coast path from Coverack. Facilities at Coverack.

Helston - Lizard Town
Coverack Bus Shelter is about 25min walk.
Map 6,B4

Coverack, Mill Beach
Most go to Mears Beach for swimming & picnicking.

Helston - St Keverne
Coverack bus shelter.
Map 6,B3

Godrevy Cove
Usually deserted beach below Roskilly's (there's hardly any parking nearby).

Helston - St Keverne
St Keverne stop then 25min walk.
Map 6,C1

Godrevy Cove

Porthoustock Cove
Pebbly beach sandwiched between quarries. Mostly used by divers exploring wrecks on the Manacles.
Ⓟ 👫
Map 6,C1

Porthallow Cove
Pebbly beach easily accessible from large beach car park.
Ⓟ 🍴 🍽 👫
Map 3,D4

Flushing, Gillan, Men-aver & Parbean Coves
No parking nearby so never busy. Good places to swim on the walk around from Porthallow.
Map 3,C3

Bosahan Cove 〰️
The first of three tiny hidden sandy beaches on the coast path between St Anthony & Helford Village. They lose the sun in late afternoon. Park at St Anthony or Helford Village. No facilities.
Map 3,B2

Helford Passage Cove
Good for small kids

Small sandy beach on north side of Helford River. Children will enjoy taking the ferry from Helford Village. Parents can sit & sip cocktails in the Ferry Boat Inn & watch the children play on the small beach. The gardens at Trebah & Glendurgan are only a 10/15min walk along the coast path.
Ⓟ 👫 🍽 🍴 👫
🚌 **Helston - Falmouth via Mawnan Smith**
Mawnan Smith, Trebah or Glendurgan stops. Steep 0.7km (½ mile) walk down to Helford Passage.
Map 3,B2

Grebe Beach 〰️
Hidden secret

One of the best small beaches in Cornwall – beautiful clear water with sparkling quartz pebbles. Take the ferry from Helford Village to Helford Passage then 15min walk along the coast path. Sun goes late afternoon.
Ⓟ at NT car park Bosloe 👫
🚌 **Helston - Falmouth via Mawnan Smith**
Jump of at Carwinion & walk down valley or follow footpath via Bosveal.
Map 3,B1

Beach safety flags

Danger – not safe to swim

Safe to swim & belly board between the flags

Area for use by surfers & windsurfers – no swimming between flags

Helford Passage

Favourite things

Beauty spots
- Carleon Cove (Map7,D1)
- Kynance Cove (7,B2)
- Housel Bay (7,C3)
- Lowland Point (6,C2)
- Flushing Cove (3,B3)

Wild & bleak
Far from the madding crowd
- Walk onto Goonhilly from Erisey (5,B3) – there are few places in Cornwall where you can taste solitude – this is one
- Trek across the downs to an isolated barrow – the downs are pretty much ignored by visitors even in the summer – pick a remote barrow & take a picnic
- Kynance North Valley – you can walk over from Kynance Gate prehistoric village or from Kynance Garage
- Loe Bar after (or during) a gale (1,C4) – the size & fury of the waves is magnificent
- The Rill & Vellan Head - when you get there you'll understand

Glendurgan

For wildlife lovers
Plants & dragonflies
The cliffs are at their best from mid-March to the end of May but the show continues into the late summer. The downs are at their best in late August & September when the heather & gorse are in flower.

Goonhilly National Nature Reserve
- Infomation boards & all the plants of serpentine heathland, just south of the Earth Station

Windmill Farm Nature Reserve (Cornwall Wildlife Trust)
- Boardwalks through wetland carr, dragonfly pools & a small information centre

Kynance Heights (7,B2)
- *Wild Thyme* & parasitic *Thyme Broomrape*

Lowland Point (6,C2)
- A mix of coastal plants, plants of wetland (*Hemlock Water Dropwort, Yellow Iris*) & around the corner *Ragged Robin*

Ancient sites
Talk with the ancestors
Kynance Gate (Map7,B2)
- Late Bronze Age Village, information board – a 10min walk from Kynance Cove

Dry Tree Goonhilly (5,C1)
- The spiritual heart of the Lizard – lots of barrows radiate along the ridges from Cruc Drænoc barrow
- Dry Tree Bronze Age menhir is nearby

Halliggye fogou at Trelowarren (2,C4)
- The best fogou in Cornwall – take a torch

Flora Day in Helston
Early each May the town dances from dawn till dusk in this famous celebration of spring. The town becomes very crowded so it's wise to arrive early. First dance starts at 7am followed by the children's dance at 10am, the main dance at midday and the final dance at 5pm. Don't miss the Hal-an-Tow Dance which starts at about 8am from the Guildhall.

GOLDEN JERSEYS
CREAM FOR SALE
SEVENTH HEAVEN
ICE CREAMS
Roskilly's

Things to do...

Visit Cornwall
Up-to-date event listings
www.visitcornwall.com

Walk + pint
For beardy beer drinkers
- New Inn at Manaccan
- Pint at the Ship Inn, Porthleven – perfect on an autumn evening after a long walk, overlooks Porthleven Harbour
- Pint at the Blue Anchor, Helston, home of Spingo Ale, one of the most popular pubs in Cornwall

Windmill Farm Nature Reserve

Adventures for smaller children...
- Helston Boating Pool & playground
- Lizard Lighthouse – climb the tower, sound the foghorn
- Helston Folk Museum is full of amazing objects
- Cornish Camels
- Flambards Fun Fair
- Beach barbecue at Cadgwith
- Roskilly's Ice Cream
- Seal Sanctuary at Gweek
- National Trust & Cornwall Wildlife Trust run sea shore safaris & rock pool

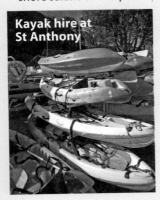

Kayak hire at St Anthony

rambles around the Helford – list of events on their websites
- Pick-your-own strawberries at the Grange Fruit Farm near Gweek, follow with pitch & putt & a meal
- Halliggye fogou (take a torch) followed by woodland walk & ice cream at the New Yard Restaurant, Trelowarren
- Trebah & Glendurgan Gardens have adventure playgrounds

Adventures for teenagers...
- Coverack Windsurf Centre, Barefoot Surf School at Gunwalloe, Poldhu Surf School
- Lizard Adventure – coasteering, kayaking, climbing and general fun
- Beach rides and trekking on the downs from Poltesco Valley Stables
- Boat hire from Helford River Boats at Helford Passage or Sailaway St Anthony
- Flambards Fun Fair
- Take a tour of Culdrose Air Base or Goonhilly

Earth Station

...for parents
- Pamper yourself at Trelowarren Spa
- Lunch at the South Cafe in Manaccan, Beach Cafe at Poldhu or at New Yard Restaurant at Trelowarren

Family day out
Flambards Fun Fair Porthleven – boats, craft shops, pasties & ice creams
Roskilly's – ice cream heaven, watch the cows being milked

When it rains
Most attractions get very busy when the weather isn't good enough for the beach, try
- Woodland walk at Frenchman's Creek and Tremayne Quay
- Flambards can get very busy when it rains or when it's overcast
- Flora Cinema in Helston – you can book tickets online at the Merlin Cinemas website
- Indoor swimming pool at Helston Sports Hall

Places to visit

Poldowrian

need to transport expectant mothers from the Isles of Scilly to the maternity ward in Truro and babies are delivered in transit.
Viewing area, shop & cafe on west side of base. Guided tours run during the season. Air day usually takes place in July. (Map 2,B3)

Helston Folk Museum
A gem. Housed in the old Butter Market. Includes cannon salvaged from the wreck of *HMS Anson* & all sorts of objects from mining and agriculture. Tremendous sense of immediacy with the exhibits.

Poldowrian
A tiny museum with prehistoric flint arrows, scrapers & pottery from nearby fields. Open on occasional days in the spring along with the garden – see Cornwall Gardens Trust & Cornwall Wildlife Trust websites. Sometimes open for a week in August. (Map5,D4)

Roskilly's
Ice cream heaven
Craft shop, cafe/restaurant, watch the cows being milked, nature trail down to Rosenithon. (Map 6,B2)

Flambards
Flumes & roller coasters
Rides for all ages, static displays of helicopters & aircraft from Culdrose next door. Very busy in school holidays – especially on overcast days. Off Sainsbury's Roundabout at Helston. (Map 2, A2)

Trelowarren
The house itself isn't open to the public but the stables and outhouses have been converted into a bistro, gallery & craft shop. Woodland walks & spa also available. (Map 2,D4)

RNAS Culdrose
Culdrose is one of the largest helicopter bases in Europe and is home to 771 Search & Rescue Squadron which patrols this part of the Cornish coast. Occasionally the squadron

Kestle Barton Gallery
Art gallery on Frenchman's Creek walk from Helford Village. (Map 3,A2)

Gardens
Most gardens shut for at least one day in the week so check opening times before you travel.
Bosahan (Map 3,B2)
☎(01326) 231351
Bonython (Map 4,D1)
☎(01326) 240550
Trebah (Map 3,B1)
☎(01326) 252200
Glendurgan (Map 3,B1)
☎(01326) 252020
Carwinion Gardens (3,C1)
☎(01326) 250258
www.gardensofcornwall.com

Lizard Lighthouse

THE LIZARD WIRELESS STATION
OPEN Please Come In
Donations Welcome

Practical advice

Hospitals
Helston Community Hospital has a Minor Injuries Unit (not 24 hours). They can deal with cuts, bruises, burns, sprains & strains. (Map 2,A2)
☎ (01326) 435815
Treliske (Truro) Hospital has a 24 hour Accident & Emergency Department
☎ (01872) 250000

Highland cattle graze the downs

Police
Helston Police Station is not open for public enquires. Nearest enquiry desks are at Falmouth, Truro & Camborne. To report a crime (non-emergency) ☎101

Adder bites
Adder bites can be painful but are not usually serious. However, the advice is to go as soon as possible to Helston MIU or Treliske (Truro) Hospital.

Supermarkets
The big supermarkets are in Helston. Mullion, Lizard Town and St Keverne have small supermarkets. Manaccan & Coverack, small general stores.

Walking on the downs
Most of the downs are open access, National Nature Reserves – we've shown them shaded on the maps. Rough tracks and fire brakes crisscross the heathland & they're the best way of getting around. It can be a difficult place to walk, particularly after rain, so wellies are a good idea, even in the summer. They give you the freedom to stride out. Otherwise it can be frustrating hopping from clump to clump going nowhere slowly.

Highland cattle
They look fierce but they're pretty docile. Best not to walk through the centre of a herd – especially if there are calves around.

Public Transport
We've added bus information to the maps but service numbers & routes do change quite frequently. Up-to-date info & timetables available at: www.cornwallpublictransport.info

Ferry contacts
Helford Ferry
Operates on-demand Easter to end October between Helford Passage & Helford Village
☎(01326) 250770
Gillan Creek Ferry
Operates on-demand Easter to end October between St Anthony & Gillan
☎(01326) 231357

You'll find lots of electric fences on the downs and cliffs. You can use these black (& sometimes orange) handles to unhook the wire & get through without electrocuting your groin.

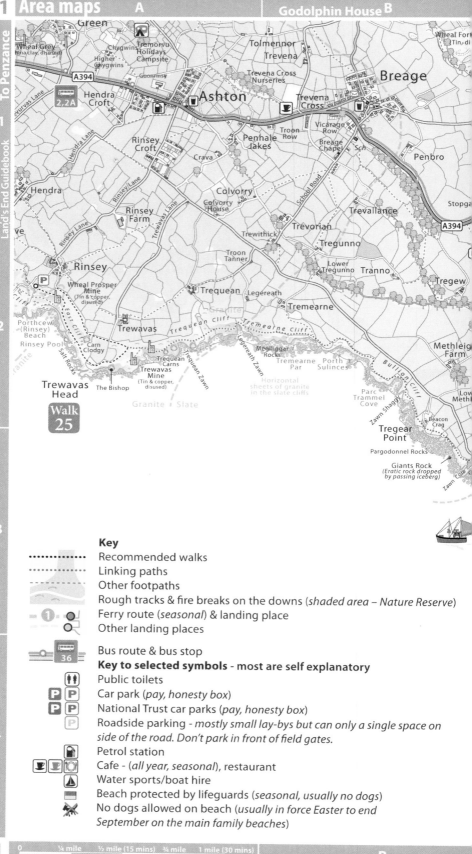

Key

••••••••••••	Recommended walks
••••••••••••	Linking paths
– – – – – –	Other footpaths
	Rough tracks & fire breaks on the downs (*shaded area – Nature Reserve*)
––**1**––○	Ferry route (*seasonal*) & landing place
○	Other landing places
==🚌== **36**	Bus route & bus stop

Key to selected symbols - most are self explanatory

🚻	Public toilets
P **P**	Car park (*pay, honesty box*)
P **P**	National Trust car parks (*pay, honesty box*)
P	Roadside parking - *mostly small lay-bys but can only a single space on side of the road. Don't park in front of field gates.*
⛽	Petrol station
⬇️ ⬇️ ◎	Cafe - (*all year, seasonal*), restaurant
⚠️	Water sports/boat hire
▭	Beach protected by lifeguards (*seasonal, usually no dogs*)
🐕	No dogs allowed on beach (*usually in force Easter to end September on the main family beaches*)

ithney

Pednavounder Farm

Mellangoose House

Mellangoose Farm
Mellangoose Mill

Grouses

Water-ma-trout Industrial Estate

Helston Sports Centre

Newham Lane

Trevarno Stream

45

Helston College

Radruith Road

B3302

39
45

Newham Farm

Helston

Station Road

A394

Sithney Common Hill

River Cober

Cober Valley

1

To Falmouth

Antron

Sithney Common

Gipsy Lane

Old Hill

Church Hill

Church St

Cross St

St Johns

Police

Godolphin Rd

Wendron St

Falm

Mus

St Elvan

Squire's Lane

Helston

Cinema

Trengrouse Way

Cricket Club

Rugby Club

Lanner Vean

Blue Anchor

Praze

Boating Lake

A394

2

Map 2

To The Lizard

2,2A

Porthleven Road

Children's Play Park

Nansloe Manor

Helston Hospital
(minor injuries, not 24hr)

Venton Vedra

Penventon

Lower Nansloe

B3304

Porthleven School

Green Lane

Higher Lanner

Loe Valley

Nansloe Farm

Degibna Lane

rthleven

Lower Lanner

Loe Marsh

Nanswidden

A3083

3

Fore St

Penrose Hill

Helston Lodge

The Loe

Degibna

Little Goonhusband

Torleven

Sunset Farm

Penrose House

Bird Hide

Higher Goonhusband

Carminow Downs Cott

P

Western Tye

Higher Penrose

Wheal Penrose Mine
(Lead, disused)

Walk 24

Degibna Wood

Chapel

Higher Pentire

Lower Goonhusband

Cviet 1884
Eastern Tye

Wheal Rose Mine
(Lead, disused)

Muddy path

Tangies

Little Nanspean

Carmin

Polcan-as Cliff

Bar Lodge

Loe Pool

Lower Pentire

Vellin-gluz Rocks

Anson 1781

Outfall

Porthleven Sands

Bar Sands

Carminowe Creek

Nanspean

Loe Bar

Tripolitania 1912

P

Clies Farm

Anson Memorial

Chyvarloe

Brankelow 1890

Berepper
Cross

Berepper

Polgre Farm

Gunwalloe

Anhay Farm

San Antonio

Chapel

Trelill

Trewennack

Gweek Lane

Grambla Farm

Woodside Farm

Grambla British Fort

St Wendron's Holy Well

Watergate

2

Boskenwyn

School

Gwealdues Hotel

Falmouth Road

Barton Farm

Trenoweth Farm

Crasken

Trewennack

Boskenwyn Manor

Walk 1

Tesco Supermarket

Pollard Farm

Boskenwyn Down

A394

Engoyse Farm

Lower Boskenwyn

Boskenwyn Prehistoric Barrow

Bosnoweth

Tregarrick

Marne Farm

Tregoon Farm

Trespison

Lower Pencoose

Mellangoose

Gweek Downs

Pollard Mill

Gay's Hill

Pemboa

Mellangoose Stream

North Goonwin

Lower Goonwin

Trevilgan Farm

Sainsburys Supermarket

Helston Downs

Flambards

Fernycombe

35

Higher Trevilgan

Nancemerrin

Zelah Farm

Royal Naval Air Station Culdrose
(HMS Seahawk)

The Grange

Fleet Air Arm
Viewing area, loos & tours

35 36 37

Rose-in-the-bush

Gilly Gabben

Treverry Farm

Main Gate

Park-an-fold

Roskymmer

Little Content Farm

Roskymmer Wood

Cottage

Culdrose Industrial Estate

B3293

Rosevear

Gunwalloe Turning

East Gate

36

Lamarth

Carminowe Wood

St Keverne Road

Tregoose Farm

Burnuick Farm

minowe

Lizard Town Road

Tregear Farm

Hendra

Merries Farm

A3083

Polwin Farm

Lower Tregiddle Farm

Higher Tregiddle Farm

Treloskan

37

Iron Age Round

Burncoose Farm

Burnow Farm

Gilly Hill

olgrean Farm

Skyburriowe

Millewarne

Penvores Farm

Belossack

Millewarne Mill

Nantithet

0.5 km   1 km   1.5 km

Gunwalloe Beach

Map 1

Mellin

Little Gilly
Wood
Polwartha

Mellingey

Naphene

Trevassack

Trengilly
Farm

Nancenoy

Polwheveral

Goongillings
Farm

Carwythenack
Farm

35

Nancenoy
Farm

Site of Iron
Age Round

Carwythenack
Round (very ruined)

Mount
View Farm

Polpenwith
Farm

Scott's Wood

Naphene
Downs

Carwythenack
Chase

Merthen Downs

Polpenwith

Scott's
Quay

Watergate
Cottage

Kestle Dee
Farm

Trethewey Downs

Polwheveral Creek

Candon
Water Farm

Lower
Carwythnack

Merthen
North Wood

North Pill

Calaman

Least
Pill

Polwhevera

Site of Iron
Age Forts

Merthen
East Wood

Seal Sanctuary

Bonallack

Cross
Cross

Merthen

Bonallack Wood

Merthen
West Wood

Tremayne Quay

Boot Yard

Lower
Quay

Merthen
Hole Quay

Tremayne

Little
Wood

Trele

Ponsontuel Creek

Helford River

West Pill

Vallum Tremayne

Middle Pill

Great Wood

**Walk
3**

Gwarth-an-drea
Plantation

Bishop's
Quay

Mawgan Creek

Mudgeon
Farm

Gwarth-an-drea

Bridge
Farm

Halanoweth

Bunnell

Mudgeon
Vean

Churchtown

Gear
Bridge

Gear Hill

Mawgan
Cross

Trelowarren
Mill

Farm
Shop

Gear

Mawgan

Mawgan
Bridge

Gear Camp
Iron Age
Enclosure

Chenhale

Carleen

Venton
Gannal

Itching
Post

Caervallack
Iron Age
Hillfort

Caervallack
Farm

Henforth

Pond
Lodge

Ten Ton
Bridge

St M

Entrance to
Trelowarren

The
Mount

Trecoose

Garras

Halliggye
Farm

Trelowarren

Colenso
Cottage

Sch

Green Hill

Lower
Garras
Farm

Halliggye Fogou
Iron Age passageway

St Martin's
Church

Barrimaylor
Farm

Gilly
Farm

Chybilly

**Walk
2**

Halliggye
Farm

Chygarkye

36

Trelowarren
Plantation

Higher
Relowas

Trethewey
Farm

Bojorrow

Trewince

Chygarkye

Exit from
Trelowarren
only

Lower
Relowas

St Martin's
Bridge

Tresize

Beeswing

Trevassack

Double
Lodges

Dobnas
Plantation

B3293

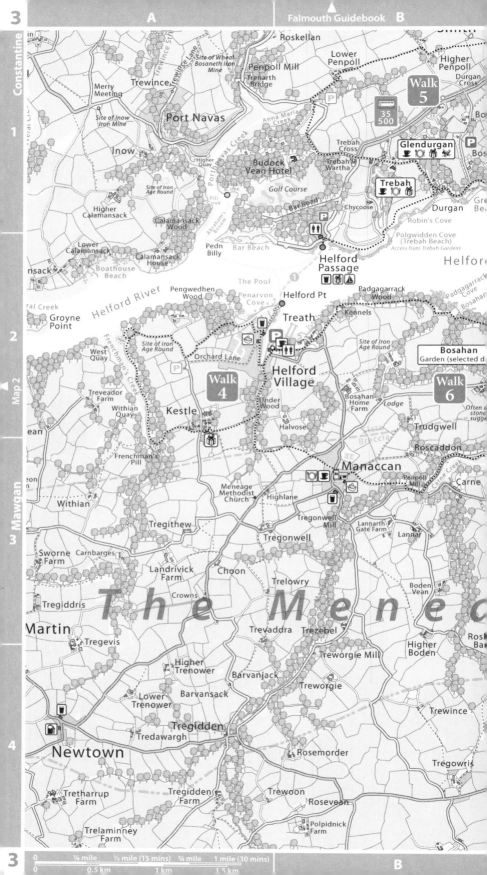

1

2

3

4

Gunwalloe

Anhay Farm

San Antonio 1527

Chyanvounder

Gunwalloe
Fishing Cove

Burgess
(abandoned)

Baulk Head

Trenoweth Farm

Chepy
(abandoned)

Park Bean Cove

Halzephron
House

Fabey's Hole

Halzephron
Cove

Toll

James &
Rebecca 1807
41 drowned

Hingey
Farm

Gunwalloe Marsh

Pedngwinian

Winnianton

Beachshop

Clubhous

Schiedam 1684

Jangye-ryn
(Fishing or
Dollar Cove)

Mullion
Golf Cours

Folded slates
in cliff

Castle Mound

Dollar Cove

*The
Towans*

Church Cove
(Gunwalloe Beach)

Carrag-a-pilez reef

Round
Barrows

SS Grip 1887

San Salvador 1669

*Jonkheer Meester Van Der
Wall Putteshock 1867*

Poldhu Cove

Poldhu Point

Marconi Centre

Men-y-grib Point

Mere
Vea

Maen Hewel

Lo Cabm

Marconi Memorial

Iris 1846

Pol Glas

Slate

Pol Brea

Polbream Poi

Polurrian C

Pe

Sandy Pec

BOUNDARY OF
LIZARD ROCKS

Rocky Pedn-y

Carrag-I

GOONHILLY BLOCK

Kissing Stone

Traboe Schist

Santa Christo De Castello 1667

Henscath

Scovarn

Mullion Cove
(Porth Mellin)

Var

Port
Py

Tregwyn

Sandy Vro

Mullion
Island

The Vro
(Gull Rock)

Pillow lava

Denise 1917

The Chair

Predann
Morv

Canavas

Maen-te-heul

Pedn Crifton

**Walk
22**

Predannack

B3293

Beeswing Trevassack

Traboe
Schist

Traboe
Cumulate

Burnoon

Dobnas
Plantation

Countybridge

Trenoweth Gwealeath
Trease

Trevassack Quarry
(serpentine, disused)

Countybridge Quarry
(serpentine, disused)

egideon
Farm

B3296 A3083

Tregaddra

'Family group'
of prehistoric
barrows

1

Skewes

Cury
Cross Lanes

Goonhilly Eart

Polglase

Bonython
Garden (selected days)

Bonython
Windfarm

Leech
Pool

Bochym
Manor

Bonython
Plantation

Dry Tree Menhir
Bronze Age standing stone

hypons

Lodge

Bochym
Enclosure

'Family group'
of prehistoric
barrows

Western
Croft

Franchis

Serpentine

Croftn

2

Higher
Bochym

Clahar
Carn

KG

Higher Bochym
Rural Workshops

Kennack
Gneiss

G o o n h i l l y D

Clahar
Garden

Carn
Maer

Fine example of
a Bronze Age
kerbed barrow

Old mine

har
ton
m

Clahar
Water

Bomb
craters

Kennack
Gneiss

Mine
Waters

Paradise
Farm

Prehistoric
barrows

W i n d m i l l
C o m m o n

Walk
15

eaver

Meaver
Crease

Prehistoric
barrows

Firebrea
rough tr

B3296

Tregullas
Farm

Trenoon

Prehisto
barrow

3

sson

Trudnoe
Farm

Penhale

Mullion
Holiday
Village

Croft
Crygar

Erisey

Kennack
Gneiss

Chybar

37

A3083

dannack Downs
life Trust Nature Reserve

Prehistoric
barrows

Prehistoric
barrows

Ponson
Joppa

Tussler's
Bridge

Chapel
Stile

Carc
Ga

Hendra

Crouder's
Bridge

Trerise

Hayle
Kimbo
Pool

Trelease

Parc-an-crouse

Walk
16

King

4

her
nnack
ws

Trelugga
Farm

Friar's Lane

Tresaddern

K

Eglos
Farm

Pons
Medda

Crowgey
Farm

Cor

k Airfield
or helicopters
Culdrose
ittance)

Ruan Major

Mount
Carlees
Farm

Long Alley

Treal

Hervan Menhir
(Bronze Age
standing stone)

Balenowe
Animal
Sanctuary

Tresize
Trewince
Trelaminney Farm
Trelease Mill
Polpidnick Farm
Polkanugga
Tregeague
An-Hay Farm
Polkerth

Traboe Cumulate (Rocks formed at the base of magma chamber)

Traboe Prehistoric Barrow Cemetery
Traboe Schist
Trenithon Farm

Carrecwynn
Green Borough Barrow

Bomb craters
Traboe Farm
Traboe
Rosuick
Grugwith

Prehistoric barrows
Access point

B3293

Cornish Camels Farm Shop

Traboe Cumulate (Rocks formed near the Moho)

Roscrowgey Farm
Roskilly

Traboe Cross

Kernewas

Croft Pascoe

Rosuic Common

B3293
Trelanvean
Zoar Garage

Croft Pascoe Pool

36

Site of Iron Age Cemetary where Trelan Mirror was discovered in 1833

Trelanvean Cross was pushed over in 1830 because of rumours that ancient gold was buried beneath it

Crousa

Barrow (2 gun ement)

Fox Covert

Access point

Trelan Gate

Trelan
Trelan Farm

Firebreaks & rough tracks (it's difficult going on this side of Goonhilly)

Middle Trelan
Lower Trelan

Peat drying platforms

'Family group' of prehistoric barrows

Heath Farm

Gabbro

Little Treleaver

Bray's Cot Pool

Serpentine

Serpentine

Ponsongath

Ponsongath Farm

Barrow Croft

Genter Farm

Gwenter

Prehistoric barrows

Treleaver Common

Access point

The Barrow

Arrowan Vean

Arrowan Common

Chiverton

Goonvean Farm

Carnpessack

Arrowan

Gwendreath Quarry (serpentine, disused)

Trevenwith Farm

Poldowrian Garden & Museum (occasional open days)

Poldowrian

Gwendreath

Wild Acres

Carn Spernic

Spernic Cove

Lankidden Cove

ver Sands liday Park

Gwendreath Holiday Park

Eastern Cliffs

Eastern Beach

Compass Cove

Ship's boiler visible at low tide

Serpentine

ampart

Kennack Towans
Caeverracks Reef

Green Saddle Rock

Carrick Lûz

Sea Acres Park

Kennack Sands
Crig-a-tanna Rocks

SS Normand 1914

The Jay

Walk 13

Serpentine
Gabbro

Kennack Sands Park

Serpentine

Lankidden Iron Age Cliff Castle

Carmar

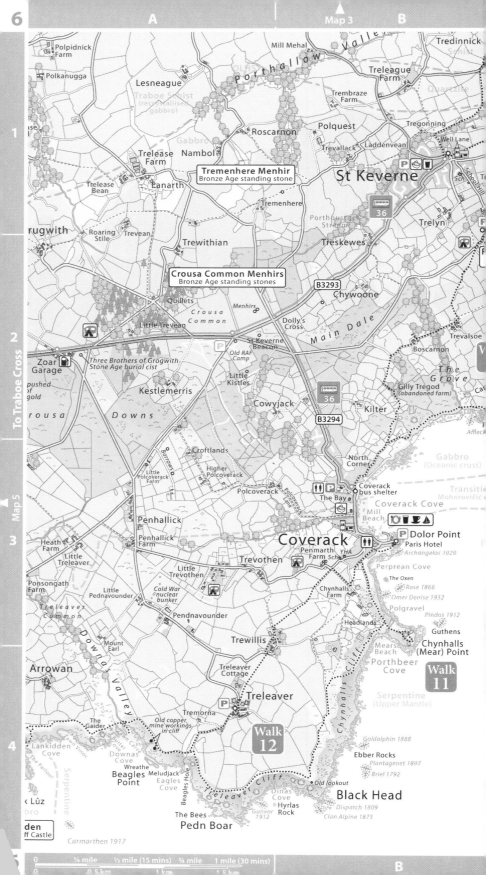

Polpidnick Farm
Polkanugga
Lesneague
Mill Mehal
Porthallow Valley
Tredinnick
Treleague Farm
Quatzite
Traboe Schist (recrystallised gabbro)
Gabbro
Roscarnon
Polquest
Tregonning
Well Lane
Trelease Farm
Nambol
Trevallack
Laddenvean
St Keverne
Sch
Trelease Bean
Lanarth

Tremenhere Menhir
Bronze Age standing stone

Tremenhere

Trelyn

rugwith
Roaring Stile
Trevean
Trewithian
Porthoustock Strand
Treskewes

Crousa Common Menhirs
Bronze Age standing stones

Quillets
Crousa Common
Menhirs
B3293
Chywoone

Little Trevean
Dolly's Cross
Main Dale

Zoar Garage
Three Brothers of Grogwith Stone Age burial cist
P
St Keverne Beacon
Old RAF Camp
Trevalsoe
Boscarnon
The Grove

pushed of gold
Kestlemerris
Little Kistles
Gilly Tregod (abandoned farm)

rousa Downs
Cowyjack
B3294
Kilter

Barrows
Croftlands
Higher Polcoverack
North Corner
Gabbro (Oceanic crust)

Little Polcoverack Farm
Polcoverack
Coverack bus shelter
Transiti
Mohorovičić
Coverack Cove

Penhallick
The Bay
Mill Beach

Penhallick Farm
Coverack
Dolor Point
Paris Hotel

Heath Farm
Little Treleaver
Trevothen
Penmarth Farm
YHA
Sch
Archangelas 1929
Perprean Cove

Ponsongath Farm
Little Pednavounder
Little Trevothen
Cold War nuclear bunker
The Oxen
Rose 1866
Omer Denise 1932

Treleaver Common
Pendnavounder
Chynhalls Farm
Polgravel
Pindos 1912

Downas Valley
Mount Earl
Trewillis
Headlands
Guthens
Chynhalls (Mear) Point

Arrowan
Treleaver Cottage
Mears Beach
Porthbeer Cove

The Gaider
Treleaver
Tremorna

Walk 11

Old copper mine workings in cliff

Walk 12

Serpentine (Upper Mantle)

Lankidden Cove
Downas Cove
Wreathe
Beagles Point
Meludjack Eagles Cove

Goldolphin 1888
Ebber Rocks
Plantagenet 1897
Briel 1792

The Parlour
Serpentine
The Bees
Pedn Boar
Gunvor 1912
Hyrlas Rock
Dinas Cove
Old lookout
Black Head
Dispatch 1809
Clan Alpine 1873

Lûz
den
ff Castle
Carmarthen 1917

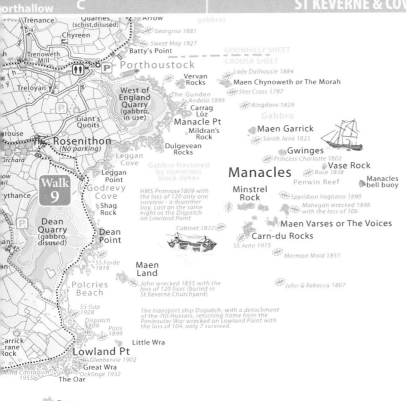

orthallow
C

Trenance
Quarries (schist, disused)
Chyreen
Arrow
Georgina 1881
Sweet May 1927
Batty's Point
GOONHILLY SHEET
CROUSA SHEET
Trenoweth Mill
Porthoustock
Vervan Rocks
Lady Dalhousie 1884
Maen Chynoweth or The Morah
Treloyan
West of England Quarry (gabbro, in use)
The Gunden
Andola 1895
Carrag Lúz
Star Cross 1787
Ringdove 1829
Gabbro
Giant's Quoits
Manacle Pt
Mildran's Rock
Maen Garrick
Sarah Jane 1823
Rosenithon
(No parking)
Dulgevean Rocks
Gwinges
Princess Charlotte 1802
Vase Rock
Rose 1838
Orchard
Leggan Cove
Gabbro fractured by numerous black dykes
Manacles
Penwin Reef
Manacles bell buoy
Leggan Point
Godrevy Cove
HMS Primrose 1809 with the loss of 120 only one survivor - a drummer boy. Lost on the same night as the Dispatch on Lowland Point
Minstrel Rock
Spyridion Vagliano 1890
Mohegan wrecked 1898 with the loss of 106
ythance
Walk 9
Shag Rock
Cabinet 1872
Maen Varses or The Voices
Dean Quarry (gabbro, disused)
Dean Point
Carn-du Rocks
SS Juno 1915
Mormon Maid 1851
SS Forde 1919
Maen Land
John wrecked 1855 with the loss of 120 lives (buried in St Keverne Churchyard)
John & Rebecca 1867
Polcries Beach
SS Gap 1928
The transport ship Dispatch, with a detachment of the 7th Hussars, returning home from the Peninsular War wrecked on Lowland Point with the loss of 104, only 7 survived.
Dispatch 1809
Paris 1899
Little Wra
Carrick Crane Rock
Lowland Pt
Glenbervie 1902
Great Wra
Ocklinge 1932
Mind Cantaquin 1955
The Oar

Davas

th Romano-British
ks. Easy to miss on
edge the remains
to evaporate salt
he Cornish Sea Salt
y do a similar
day at Porthkerris.

Downs

Predannack Manor

Teneriffe Farm

Walk 22

Predannack Wollas

Windyridge Farm

Predannack Airfield
Training area for helicopters
from RNAS Culdrose
(No admittance)

*Hervan Menhir
(Bronze Age
standing stone)*

*Anti-
Ba*

*L o w e r
P r e d a n n a c k
D o w n s*

Parc Bean Cove
Ogo-dour Cove

Predannack Cliff

hist
umulate
)

Dog Brook

Ro
the

*Dragonfly
ponds*

Pol Cornick
Velvet Rock

*Nature
Trails*

Wind
Far

George's
Cove

Serpentine

Walk 21

*Old fighter jets &
helicopters used
for rescue practice*

*Wetland
boardwalks*

Windmill Farm
Nature Reserve

Vellan
Head

*Stromboli
1878*

Gersick-an-zawn

Kynance
Farm

Access
point

*Permissive path
linking Lizard Downs
& Windmill Farm
Nature Reserve*

Groc
F

Pengersick

*Prehistoric
barrow on
skyline*

Ogo Pons
Gew-graze
(Soapy Cove)

*Old Quarry
(soap rock/
steatite)*

*Kissing
gate*

Kynance Gate
Prehistoric Village

Pigeon Ogo

Kynance

Kynance Brook

*Dead
end
path*

The Horse

Kynance Cliff

*Firebreak
& rough
tracks*

Walk 20

*Kynance
North Valley*

L i z a r d

The Pound

The Rill

Kynance
Heights

Kynance So

Rill Point

*Lawarnick
Pit*

Tor Balk

Rill Ledges

*Abernyfe
1898*

Rill
Cove

Lawarnick
Cove

Pentreath Cliff

Ca
G

Asparagus Island
The Devil's Letterbox
Gull Rock

**Kynance
Cove**

Yellow
Carn

Holestrow

The Bishop

Lion Rock

Enys
Vean

Serpentine

Maud 1912
Boiler visible at low tide

Cae

GOONHILLY SHEET

MAN O' WAR SHEET
500 million year old rocks that predate
the creation of the Rheic Ocean

Pentreath
Beach

Landewednack Schist
(recrystallised pillow lava & basalt)

Caerthillian
Cove

Crane Ledges

Holseer Cove

Old Lizard Head
Schists
(recrystallised ocean
sediments)

Scathe
Venton Hill Point

Suffolk 1866

Old Lizard Head

Clank

Xonthus 1841
Quadrant

HMS Royal Anne 1721
Queen Margret 1913

Mulvin   Stags

Taylor's Rock
Eltyenburgh 1854

Man of War Gneiss & grani
(Heavily deformed granite rock
from the Gondwanian plate tha
crashed into Cornwall)

0   ¼ mile   ½ mile (15 mins)   ¾ mile   1 mile (30 mins)
0.5 km   1 km

Pons Medda
Long Alley
Bolenowe Animal Sanctuary
Bonadventure
Sunny Corner
chapel
Crowgey Farm
Treveddon Farm
Treal
Kuggar
Corgerrick
Came
Walk 16
Polstangey Farm
Poltesco Farm
Mill
Poltesco
Treleague
Treleague Crossroads
Carleon
Friar's Lane
Kennack Sands Park
Sea Acres Park
Kennack Sands
Crig-a-tanna Rock
Serpentine
Cavouga Rocks
Polbream Pt
Serpentine
Little Cove
Todden
Poltesco Rock
Carleon (Poltesco) Cove
Black Rock
Serpentine
Walk 17

Little Trethvas
Worvas Farm
St Ruan
Bruggan
Ruan Minor
Sch
SS Highland Fling 1907
Ledgeventon Rocks
Enys Head
Brandise
Kildown Cove
Signal Staff Quarry (serpentine, disused)
Kildown Point
GOONHILLY SHEET
MAN O'WAR SHEET
500 million year old rocks that predate the creation of the Rheic Ocean

New Road
Steep, narrow road (avoid in summer)
Mile End
Chyheira Farm
St Ruan's Well
Medieval Holy Well
Cadgwith
Terrick
The Colt
Huers Hut
Fishing Cove
The Todden
Little Cove (Swimming Cove)
Devil's Frying Pan (Collapsed cave)

Anvoaze
St Grada's Church
Gwavas Vean
Prazegooth
Ynyswidden
Dollar Ogo
Chough's Ogo
Carn Barrow
SS Socoa stranded 1906
Schist crags & cliffs
Gwavas Farm
Serpentine
Polgwidden
Polbarrow Arch
SS Bellucia 1917
Craggan Rocks
Schist, gabbro & Kennack gneiss make up a narrow coastal fringe

Trethvas Farm
A3083
37
Kynance Cove Turn
Lizard Town
Whale Rock
Parn Voose Cove
Balk Quarry (serpentine, disused)
The Balk
Church Cove
Battleship Rock
Kilcobben Cove
Lizard Lifeboat Station
Prilla Cove
Hot Point
Hot Cove
Adolf Vinnen 1923
Pyg
Clan Malcolm 1935
Tregurra
SS Mosel 1882
Bass Point
Coastwatch Lookout
Lloyd's Signal Station
Cromdale 1913
Spernan Shoals

Landewednack
Cross Common
Cross
Tregaminion
Walk 18
Lizard Wireless Station
Old Nuclear Bunker
Housel Bay
Pen Olver
Hansy 1911
Vrogue Rock
Czar 1859

Chapel Lane
Walk 19
Lloyd's Lane
Lizard Bay Road
Lizard Point
Laven-a-cean
Bolijack
Daws Ogo
Lion's Den Cave
Bumble Cove
Bumble Rock
Lizard Lighthouse
Arab 1888
Gypsy Queen 1887
Labham Reef
Pen Ervan
Enoch Rock
Nuovo Raffaelino 1872
Wandsbek 1900
Pelicanos 1853
The Dales
Mên Hyr
Suevic 1907
Landewednack Schist (recrystallised pillow lava & basalt)
Old Lizard Head Schists (recrystallised ocean sediments)

Northbroad/Penmenner Rd

1 2 3

					Buses, bus stops & ferry links
		☐ Easy ☐ Moderate ☐ SAS			
1. The Helford River & Meneage	**1**	Gweek & Merther Uny	11km (7 miles) 4–5 hours		🚌 **Helston–Falmouth bus (35)** Gweek stop at bottom of walk. 🚌 **Helston – Falmouth bus (2)** Trevenen stop on A394 at top of wa...
	2	Trelowarren Woods *Open 1 April to 30 Sept only*	6.5km (4 miles) 2–3 hours		🚌 **Helston–Lizard bus (37)** Nearest stop Garras Methodist Chu... 2.2km (1¼ miles) walk to Trelowarr... along driveway past Halliggye fog...
	3	Tremayne Quay Stroll	4km (2½ miles) 1–2 hours		No bus service
	4	Frenchman's Creek Stroll	4km (2½ miles) 1–2 hours		No bus service
	5	Helford Gardens – Trebah, Carwinion & Glendurgan	6.5km (4 miles) 2–3 hours via Penpoll		Helford ferry runs from Helford Vill... to Helford Passage, Easter to end ... October ☎ (01326) 250770. 🚌 **Helston–Falmouth bus (35)**
	6	Helford, Manaccan & St Anthony	7.3km (4½ miles) 2–3 hours		Gillan Creek ferry runs from St Antho... to the Gillan side of Carne Creek in ... summer to link with Walk 7. ☎ (01326) 231357
	7	Porthallow, Gillan, Flushing & Nare Point	6.5km (4 miles) 2–3 hours		🚌 **Helston–St Keverne bus (36)** Nearest stop St Keverne Square 1.7... (1 mile) from Porthallow.
	8	Quarry Walk – St Keverne, Porthallow & Porthoustock	6.5km (4 miles) 2–3 hours		🚌 **Helston–St Keverne bus (36)** St Keverne Square stop, path leave... from churchyard.
	9	Roskilly's Stroll	3.1km (2 miles) 1–2 hours		🚌 **Helston–St Keverne bus (36)** St Keverne Square stop then walk ... Roskilly's along Trelyn Lane.
	10	Lowland Point	8.2km (5 miles) 3–4 hours		🚌 **Helston–St Keverne bus (36)** Coverack bus shelter, North Corner stop.
2. The Far South	**11**	Chynhalls Stroll from Coverack	2.6km (1½ miles) 1–2 hours		🚌 **Helston–St Keverne bus (36)** Coverack bus shelter, North Corner stop.
	12	Coverack, Black Head & Downas Cove	6.3km (4 miles) 3–4 hours		🚌 **Helston–St Keverne bus (36)** Coverack bus shelter, North Corner 4 car park spaces at Treleaver.
	13	Kennack Sands to Lankidden Cove	4.7km (3 miles) 1–2 hours		🚌 **Helston–Lizard bus (37)** Kuggar stop. 🚌 **Helston–St Keverne bus (36)** Coverack bus shelter, North Corner stop.

walks in this book

Food & drinks	Notes
& 🍴 Gweek, onstantine & ngilly Wartha	Follows the river valleys north and west of Gweek up to the edge of the Carnmenellis granite. At Merther Uny a Romano-British *round* has been reused as an early Christian sanctuary. Far from the madding crowd. Easily split into smaller walks.
& 🍴 Trelowarren & d Court House, Mawgan	Circular walks through the woods of Trelowarren Estate. You can extend to take in Tremayne Quay on the river (Walk 3). Trelowarren has parking, cafe/restaurant, art gallery & craft centre.
& 🍴 Trelowarren & d Court House, Mawgan	Lovely walk to the Helford. Great at any time of year. Parking is restricted to 2 or 3 places at the side of the road – in the summer, it's probably best to park at Trelowarren & follow Walk 2.
& 🍴 Helford Village	A very popular & atmospheric walk from Helford Village to the creek that inspired Daphne Du Maurier's novel, good for kids (there's an old wreck to look at).
& 🍴 lford Passage, the gardens & awnan Smith	A short ferry ride across the Helford River to the sub-tropical gardens on the north bank of the Helford. Or alternatively, a walk to Rosemullion Head Mawnan Smith or Penpoll.
& 🍴 Helford Village & Manaccan	The final part of the Helford estuary before you reach open sea, returning along Gillan Creek & taking in the three prettiest villages in the Meneage.
& 🍴 Porthallow & t Apple Cafe at ark-an-tidno	Rarely busy walk (the only parking is at Porthallow) with views over Falmouth Bay. Mix of sheltered estuary & open cliff. Nare Head was a decoy site in World War 2. Gillan Creek is outstanding.
& 🍴 n St Keverne, Porthallow & ark-an-tidno	Follows the old paths that connect St Keverne to the coastal villages of Porthoustock & Porthallow. Then along the unofficial coast path through the old cliff top quarries.
& 🍴 At Roskilly's	From Roskilly's, past wildlife pools to Godrevy beach overlooking the Manacles. Bring food for the ducks & end with a Roskilly's ice cream.
& 🍴 n Coverack & at Roskilly's	A riot of wild flowers in spring & summer. Picnic at Carrick Crane Crags & then up to Roskilly's for tea or ice cream & back through a deserted farmstead to Coverack. Plant lover's treat.
& 🍴 In Coverack	A short stroll from Coverack to the Iron Age Cliff Castle at Chynhalls. Picnic inside the ramparts of the old cliff castle. Swim at Mears beach.
& 🍴 In Coverack	Builds up to the high cliffs at Black Head & Pedn Boar. If the tide is right, a sandy beach is uncovered at Downas Cove for a few hours – a good spot for a picnic.
& Kennack Sands & in Coverack	South-facing cliffs & a cliff castle. Reach here either from Kennack Sands (nearest) or Coverack. Beach at Lankidden gets sun in the morning (unofficial Naturist beach). Spernic & Compass coves aren't accessible from coast path. Can be difficult going after rain.

		Easy ☐ Moderate ☐ SAS ☐	Distance/time	Buses, bus stops & ferry links
2. The Far South	14	Goonhilly Downs, Dry Tree stroll	4km (2½ miles) 1–2 hours	🚌 **Helston–St Keverne bus (3** Goonhilly Earth Station stop National Nature Reserve & car p is just south of Earth Station.
	15	Goonhilly & Erisey	8.8km (5½ miles) 3–4 hours	🚌 **Helston–St Keverne bus (3** Goonhilly Earth Station stop National Nature Reserve & car p is just south of Earth Station
	16	Erisey, Poltesco & Carleon Cove	5.8km (3½ miles) 2–3 hours	🚌 **Helston–Lizard bus (37)** Ask to get off at Polstangey Bric
	17	Poltesco Stroll	1.6km (1 mile) 1 hour	🚌 **Helston–Lizard bus (37)** Ruan Minor stop & walk dow Poltesco Lane
	18	Landewednack, Housel Bay & Lizard Point	5km (3 miles) 1–2 hours	🚌 **Helston–Lizard bus (37)** Tregaminion or Lizard Green st
	19	Lizard Point, Pentreath & Kynance Cove	7km (4¼ miles) 2–3 hours	🚌 **Helston–Lizard bus (37)** Lizard Green stop or jump off Kynance Garage & walk acros Lizard Downs.
	20	Kynance, The Rill & Gew-graze (Soapy Cove)	3km (2 miles) 1–2 hours	🚌 **Helston–Lizard bus (37)** Lizard Green stop or jump off Kynance Garage & walk acros Lizard Downs (both add 2km)
	21	Predannack, Vellan Head & Soapy Cove	4km (2½ miles) 1–2 hours	Nearest is 🚌 **Helston–Lizard bus (37)** Mullion Cricket Club stop, then ; walk to Predannack Wollas.
	22	Predannack Head, Ogo-dour & Mullion Cove	5km (3 miles) 2–3 hours	🚌 **Helston–Lizard bus (37)** Mullion Cricket Club stop.
3. West Coast	23	Halzephron, Gunwalloe & Cury Churchtown	5.5km (3½ miles) 2–3 hours	🚌 **Helston–Lizard bus (37)** Mullion Golf Club or Poldhu, wa Gunwalloe, Halzephron and picl bus again at Cury Churchtow
	24	Loe Bar & Pool	8.7km (5½ miles) 3–4 hours	🚌 **Helston–Penzance bus (2,2** Penrose Hill or Porthleven Rd st
	25	Trewavas Head & Rinsey	2.6km (1½ miles) 1–2 hours	Nothing close but you could get 🚌 **Helston–Penzance bus (2,2** & get off at the Lion & Lamb a Ashton. Then 2km (1¼ mile) wa to Rinsey hamlet, & walk back Porthleven on coast path.

Food & drinks	Notes
☕ & 🍴 earest is New d Restaurant at Trelowarren	Info boards on wildlife of the downs plus the remains of the World War 2 radar station. Level paths OK for wheelchairs & buggies. Best in late summer for flowering heath, always difficult going after rain (summer or winter) so bring wellies.
☕ & 🍴 earest is New d Restaurant at Trelowarren	This is a bit of an epic journey – it's almost invariably boggy. A walk across the huge barrow cemetery on Goonhilly Downs, turning off to follow the valley to Erisey & connect with the walk down to Carleon Cove on the coast (Walk 16). Bring wellies.
☕ & 🍴 los Farm near Ruan Major	Carleon Cove is many people's favourite Lizard beauty spot. Walk from the sea to the edge of Goonhilly Downs.
☕ & 🍴 Nearest is Cadgwith, ennack Sands	A short walk around the beautiful Carleon Cove from the National Trust car park. You could keep walking around to Cadgwith for lunch & come back on the coast path cutting back up Friar's Lane & Poltesco Lane.
☕ & 🍴 Lizard Town, Lizard Point, usel Bay Hotel	The most handsome cliffs on the Lizard, lush & green in the summer. Housel Bay is outstanding. You could extend this walk to include Old Lizard Head & Pentreath.
☕ & 🍴 Lizard Town, izard Point & ynance Cove	Perhaps the most popular walk in this book. Spectacular variety of cliffs and different rock types. Kynance Cove is outstanding. In early summer cliffs are cloaked in flowers – a plant lover's treat.
☕ & 🍴 Kynance Cove Cafe	Magnificent raw serpentine cliffs. Less busy than the very popular walk to Kynance from Lizard Town, but actually more spectacular. Prehistoric Village at Kynance Heights. Links to Windmill Farm Nature Reserve.
☕ & 🍴 arest is Mullion lage & Mullion Meadows	Impressive, savage cliffs in all weathers – a real taste of the serpentine landscape. Links to walk from Kynance Cove. Picnic on the Rill. Bring wellies.
☕ & 🍴 arest is Mullion lage & Mullion Meadows	Spectacular cliffs – the highest on the Lizard. Bring binoculars to watch seals & seabirds on Mullion Island & the Vro. Orchids on Mullion Cliff in spring & summer.
☕ & 🍴 Halzephron n, beach shop at Gunwalloe, lzephron House renoweth Farm	Gentle walk around the back of Gunwalloe Marsh. The footpath crosses the marshes on boardwalks. Not really a circular walk (the road between Cury and Poldhu is narrow & busy), but you could jump off the bus at Cury Church, walk to Halzephron for lunch & then pick the bus up again at Poldhu.
☕ & 🍴 afe at Helston ating Pool or in Porthleven	Really popular walks around Loe Pool. Most people do one side or the other. The eastern side is quieter. The western side follows the old driveway from Helston to Penrose so it's good for kids on bikes & you can get a buggy along it too. Walks of all sizes
☕ & 🍴 ubs at Ashton Breage, cafe Trevena Cross Nurseries	Impressive granite cliffs & beautiful sandy cove at Rinsey (covered on a high tide). Could walk from Porthleven along the coast path – it's about 4km (2½ miles). Natural pool for diving & swimming at East Cliff near Rinsey.

Index